The
Silversmiths of Kentucky
1785 to 1850

SILVER PATEN

Paten 4¼" high, 6" in diameter, made by William and Archabald Cooper of Louisville and Frankfort. Owned by Mr. and Mrs. Noble W. Hiatt.

The Silversmiths of Kentucky
1785 to 1850

NOBLE W. HIATT & LUCY F. HIATT

COMMONWEALTH BOOK COMPANY
St. Martin, Ohio

ORIGINALLY PUBLISHED BY THE AUTHORS
IN 1954 IN A NUMBERED, LIMITED EDITION
OF 1000 COPIES

THIS EDITION IS LIMITED
TO 250 COPIES

© 2016 by Commonwealth Book Company
St. Martin, Ohio

ISBN: 978-1-948986-38-0

All rights reserved. No part of this book may be reproduced in any form or by any means without the prior written consent of the publisher, excepting brief quotes used in reviews.
Printed in the United States of America.

To

J. Winston Coleman, Jr., Litt.D.

Whose advice and friendship have been an endless source of help and encouragement.

Contents

	PAGE
FRONTISPIECE	ii
ILLUSTRATIONS	vii
ABBREVIATIONS	viii
INTRODUCTION	xix
PREFACE	xiii
SILVERSMITHS OF KENTUCKY	1
UNCONFIRMED LIST OF KENTUCKY SILVERSMITHS	103
SKETCHES OF MARKS	111
BIBLIOGRAPHY	119
INDEX	127

Illustrations

PATEN MADE BY WILLIAM AND ARCHABALD COOPER..........*Frontispiece*
    Owned by Mr. and Mrs. Noble W. Hiatt
    (Photograph by Max Galloway Studio)

                                                                                                                            PAGE

LARGE SHELL BOWL SPOON MADE BY JAMES P. BARNES.............. 9
    Owned by Mr. and Mrs. John W. Luckett
    (Photograph by Max Galloway Studio)

LARGE LADLES MADE BY ASA BLANCHARD..................... 15
    One ladle owned by J. Winston Coleman, Jr.
    One ladle owned by William H. Townsend
    (Photograph by Lafayette Studio)

FOOTED SILVER CUPS MADE BY GARNER AND WINCHESTER......... 35
    Owned by J. Winston Coleman, Jr.
    (Photograph by Lafayette Studio)

SILVER CUPS MADE BY JOHN KITTS, HUDSON AND DOLFINGER,
    HENRY HUDSON, AND JOHN B. AKIN........................... 53
    Owned by Katherine Wakefield Gilliatt (Mrs. C. E.)
    (Photograph by J. Sheets)

1832 LEMON AND KENDRICK LEDGER........................... 57
    Owned by William Kendrick Jewelers, Inc.
    (Photograph by Louisville Courier-Journal Staff Photographer)

1838 MARSH LEDGER... 61
    Owned by Miss Jane Marsh
    (Photograph by Max Galloway Studio)

DAVID A. SAYRE... 77
    From a portrait. Sayre School, Lexington

PITCHER AND TRAY MADE BY GEORGE W. STEWART............. 93
    Owned by Victor Bogaert Jewelry Company
    (Photograph by Lafayette Studio)

ABBREVIATIONS

b.—born
d.—died
w.—working
c.—circa
a.—apprenticed

Introduction

THE MARK of the tomahawk was still fresh on forest trees when early travelers to Kentucky noted with surprise the exquisite silverware on the frontier. Some of it, no doubt, had been carried by pack-horses across the hazy Alleghenies from Virginia and the Carolinas, but the records show that most of it was the handiwork of local craftsmen.

As early as 1785, Joshua Humphreys and Edward West were busy in their shops in Lexington. A few years later, T. K. and B. B. Marsh, and Alexander and Robert Frazer in the neighboring town of Paris; Felix F. Cachot and Jonathan Simpson, of Bardstown; Richard E. Smith, James I. Lemon and William Kendrick, of Louisville, together with Samuel Ayres and Asa Blanchard—the most famous of them all —were hammering out gleaming handwrought masterpieces of silverware. Many of these articles today are precious heirlooms, still in the proud possession of descendants of the original owners who lived in "stately, elegant, costly brick mansions," so much admired by English and French visitors to the Western Country. Since "coin" silverware was a mark of gentility and elegance, it is only natural that Lexington, the "Athens of the West," should have been the center of this industry.

The term "coin silver" derived its name from the fact that most of this metal came from melted money—English, French, Mexican, Spanish and some of the scarce American coins—dollars, half-dollars, piasters and other denominations. Usually, it took one silver dollar to make a teaspoon, and although the finished products carried no definite standard guarantee, it was generally understood that "coin quality" was rated at about 825/1000, which meant that the product contained 825 parts of pure silver to 175 parts of alloy.

The silver flatware and hollowware—beautiful and often fragile— which took shape under the skillful hands of these pioneer Kentucky craftsmen, were wide in pattern and variety. There were teaspoons, dessert spoons, tablespoons, ladles, sugar tongs, butter knives, casters, cups, pitchers, trays, tea sets with receptacles for cream and sugar and waste, and even articles of personal adornment, such as breast pins and rings. The silversmiths usually worked by special order. The head of the household would visit his shop with pockets sagging with silver dollars, a list of articles desired and a rough sketch or description of pattern or design. However, some shops kept a small stock of the customary silverware "made up" and ready for sale. These pieces frequently consisted of cups, spoons and other articles suitable for prizes at stock shows and agricultural fairs and many of these

Introduction

"premium cups," in after years, became rare and famous as mint julep cups.

Early town directories and other records show that most silversmiths had their shops at fixed and prominent locations. Some, however, like the early itinerant cobbler or shoemaker traveled from house to house, boarding with customers while their corner cupboards and cutlery chests were being replenished and enriched by the now priceless objects that came from crucible, mallet and anvil. Fortunately, unlike Jouett, Frazer and other early Kentucky portrait painters, most of the silversmiths identified their handiwork by stamping their names and oftentimes the place of manufacture on the underside of the bowl or spoon. Asa Blanchard, on occasion, would stamp an eagle with outspread wings as an additional mark of identification, but only a few followed his example in this respect.

According to the custom of highly skilled crafts, silversmithing obtained its recruits by the apprentice system. A young man who wanted to learn the trade, as many court records show, pledged himself under a rigid apprentice bond to the service of an established silversmith for a term frequently as long as seven years. In return for being taught the "mystery of silversmithing," the apprentice received lodging, food and clothing and at the end of his term of service, a suit of clothes and $50 in cash.

During the first era of the nineteenth century, the silversmith prospered greatly. Frequently he became a man of considerable wealth and prominence in the community. Like Lexington's David A. Sayre, some entered the fields of banking and philanthropy. Others, like Edward West, tried their hand at inventions, while still others expanded their business until they became general merchants or "full line jewelers." But, as years went by, the silversmith fell a victim of the machine age. About 1840, Newell Harding, of Boston, invented a machine for rolling out silverware and shaping it, which gradually made the old handwrought method obsolete and unprofitable. Within a decade, more of the "old masters" had retired from business and were almost forgotten.

The present volume is highly informative and interesting, and shows the results of years of unflagging study and research on the part of its authors. Spurred on by the realization that they were digging in virgin soil, they visited museums, sought out heirloom treasures in private homes, unearthed old family letters, account books and other records, pored over advertisements in musty newspaper files and interviewed aged individuals whose lives and memories ran back into the colorful era of silversmithing.

And so it is that from the buried years of a picturesque, bygone industry, the authors are now able to resurrect and present to their readers in the forthcoming pages no less than two hundred and forty-

Introduction

four silversmiths who have been definitely identified as Kentucky craftsmen. They also list the names of thirty-one other men who are not positively identified as Kentucky craftsmen.

This work, compiled with meticulous care, attractive in illustrations and format, is a "must" for antique dealers and collectors, and will also have a wide appeal to historians and all other persons interested in Kentuckiana and Americana.

J. WINSTON COLEMAN, JR.

Winburn Farm

Lexington, Kentucky

Preface

KENTUCKY has been a part of my life since my earliest childhood. My mother's family came to Kentucky and the Ohio Valley from Virginia, and many of my ancestors served Kentucky as doctors and educators. How well I remember the many happy experiences with my family in Kentucky—experiences which have become a part of my lifelong memories. There was the very special flavor of the large red apples. Wood smoke in the early morning was mixed with the tantalizing aroma of frying ham, biscuits and boiling coffee as it was wafted onto the wood porch where the trellis was heavy with honeysuckle. There were the board walks, the ponds where we fished so hopefully, the wonderful family reunions, the springs at Sebree, childhood friends, and my grandfather's office where he practiced dentistry—these and countless other early memories of Kentucky are mine to enjoy.

My husband and I have been entranced with another picture of Kentucky. We have enjoyed the food, comfort and service of Kentucky's fine hotels as well as the quaint inns which have their own special charm. We have become acquainted with many residents of Kentucky, and as a result have made many wonderful new friends to enrich our lives. In no other state have we encountered such a delightful interest in our hobby—early American silver. As we have searched for information dealing with the early silversmiths of the State of Kentucky we have been accorded the most generous assistance on every hand. So many Kentucky residents have opened their doors to us and shared with us their knowledge of these early craftsmen. We have searched long and worked hard, but all through the years we have spent in securing additional data concerning these early artists there were those whose interest did not lag and who continued to be of great assistance. We feel deeply grateful to the generous and gracious folk of Kentucky.

Special acknowledgment is made to Mr. Bayless Hardin, Secretary of the Kentucky Historical Society in Frankfort; Miss Virginia Hayes, Librarian, Lexington Public Library; the Transylvania College Library staff; the University of Kentucky Library staff; Miss Mary Verhoeff, Vice-President of The Filson Club in Louisville and her assistants; the personnel of the Kentucky Room of the Louisville Public Library; the Indianapolis Public Library and the staff in the Genealogy Room of the Indiana State Library, for their courtesy in placing their records and facilities at our disposal.

Mr. Richard Allison, Superintendent of the Lexington Cemetery, together with Mrs. Allison, generously made available to us the ex-

Preface

cellent records there. Information was also obtained from the records of the Cave Hill Cemetery of Louisville.

Mr. William Penton Kendrick and Mr. William Kendrick Ewing of William Kendrick Jewelers, Inc., in Louisville graciously gave of their time, knowledge and records, as did Mrs. Brainard Lemon, Mr. John L. Milton and Mr. Demaree of Lemon and Son in Louisville.

County Court Clerks all over Kentucky were co-operative and kind in their assistance, and we gratefully acknowledge their help.

We are also indebted to many individuals not necessarily connected with any organization, library or society, who readily gave of their time in research, their own personal records, knowledge and libraries as well as their experience, in many instances, as authors in their own right. To the following people we owe a tremendous debt of gratitude: Dr. J. Winston Coleman, Jr., Mr. William H. Townsend, Mr. Charles R. Staples, Mr. Victor Bogaert, Jr., and Miss Elizabeth Steele of Lexington; Miss Jane Marsh and Mrs. Julia S. Ardery of Paris; over a period of many months Mrs. Wade Hampton Whitley of Paris has given generously of her time, records and information concerning many of the early Kentucky craftsmen; Mrs. C. E. Gilliatt of Seymour, Indiana; Mrs. Charlton Alexander of Versailles; Mrs. Shelby S. Van Hoy, Jr., and J. S. Chandler of Campbellsville; Miss Nannie K. Starling of Hopkinsville; Miss Mabel Weaks and Miss Lucy A. Ditto of Louisville; Mrs. Eleanor Hume Offutt of Frankfort; Mr. and Mrs. John W. Muir, Mrs. Rebecca Talbott, Mayor and Mrs. Frank B. Wilson and Miss Gertrude Smith of Bardstown; the late Dr. and Mrs. Walter E. Wright of "Wickland," Bardstown; Mrs. Charles William Newman and Mr. and Mrs. John W. Luckett of Indianapolis, Indiana; Mrs. Lula Reed Boss of Maysville; Dr. Edward Callistus Barlow, Mrs. Brice M. Goldsborough and Mrs. John Pack of Georgetown; Mr. Rankin Kirkland of Paducah; Mr. and Mrs. W. B. Jones, Jacksonville, Illinois; Mrs. John D. Wakefield of Norfolk, Virginia, and Mrs. Robert Whitfield Miles, Principal of Sayre School, Lexington, Kentucky.

No effort has been made herein to describe the methods employed by the early silversmiths. This is a subject which has been covered specifically and well in other books dealing with early American silver and its makers. We have attempted to compile as much pertinent data concerning each Kentucky workman as possible—when and where he worked, his family, and his place in the community. In some few instances there was such a wealth of material that it was deemed necessary to omit a great deal of the less pertinent information, while just the opposite has been true in many cases wherein only a little information could be found.

We have shown some of the makers' marks in this work in order to illustrate the typical markings found on silver made and sold in Kentucky. Almost all of Kentucky's silversmiths used their last name.

Preface

alone or with their initials, which makes identification of the silversmith or jeweler a simple matter. The work of many of these smiths is extremely rare and no examples have been seen by the authors. Jewelers, especially in the Louisville area, have been included in this work. There is a great deal of silver which carries the mark of a jeweler. Sometimes silver was made in the jeweler's shop by silversmiths employed for that purpose; sometimes silver was ordered from a silversmith and the silver marked with the name of the jeweler for whom it was intended. In some cases, silversmiths who did a prosperous business found it impossible to make enough silver to supply the demands of their customers, in which case the silver was made elsewhere and stamped with the name of the local silversmith. Peter L. Krider of Philadelphia made a great deal of silver for various silversmiths in Kentucky. Further, known silversmiths were frequently carried in the directories as jewelers as well as watch- and clockmakers. There is also one known instance of a jeweler being carried in a directory as a silversmith. Insofar as possible, we have designated whether a workman was a jeweler or a silversmith in actual fact, but by listing both we have attempted to identify the source, if not the actual maker, of most of the silver originating in Kentucky.

Included in this volume is a list of men who are purported by some to have been Kentucky silversmiths. We have been unable to verify, with certainty, the contention that they were Kentucky silversmiths and, therefore, they are listed in a separate group. Continued searching may one day bring new facts to light concerning some of these men, either proving or disproving their rightful place among the silversmiths of Kentucky.

Listed individually and alphabetically are those men or firms who were in business before 1850. Many of them continued in business for many years after 1850, and in such cases some information is given concerning their later business activities.

Data for this work has been gleaned from many sources, and every effort has been made to avoid errors. Insofar as records and information have been available, this work is accurate and factual and includes a number of early Kentucky craftsmen who had not been previously identified.

Only a few of the early silversmiths of Kentucky have been included in the many books previously published concerning early American silver and its makers. It is the earnest hope of the authors that this book will be informative and helpful to those interested in the beautiful work of the early craftsmen and the part they played in the history and development of the State of Kentucky.

Lucy F. Hiatt

111 Bow Lane
Indianapolis, Indiana
January 25, 1954

ADAIR, R. F.

w. 1796 or before—Paris

1796—Lexington

R. F. Adair, one of the early silversmiths of Kentucky, moved from Paris to Lexington in 1796, or shortly thereafter. He made some of the early silver service for the Phoenix Hotel in Lexington.

ADAMS, C. J.

w. 1840—Frankfort

Very little has been found concerning this craftsman other than the fact that he worked in Frankfort.

AKIN, JOHN B.

1820-1860—Danville

John B. Akin, also known as "Brent" Akin, silversmith, worked in Danville. His father was William Akin, another early Kentucky silversmith.

Many pieces of his silver are still to be found. Katherine Wakefield Gilliatt (Mrs. C. E.) of Seymour, Indiana, owns a butter knife and a sugar shell each marked "J. B. AKIN." A sister of Mrs. Wade Hampton Whitley of Paris owns a cup marked "JOHN B. AKIN" "STANDARD" "★P.L.K.★." This last mark is interesting in view of the fact that the piece was actually made by Peter L. Krider of Philadelphia for John B. Akin, as were six silver cups owned by Mrs. John Pack of Georgetown marked "JOHN B. AKIN" "DANVILLE, KY.," and marked in addition, variously, "STANDARD" "P.L.K.," "P. L. KRIDER" "PHILA. PA." and "P. L. KRIDER" "PHILA. PA." "STANDARD."

AKIN, WILLIAM

w. 1812-1820—Danville

d. 1824—Fredericktown, Maryland

William Akin, silversmith, worked in Danville, as did his son, John B. Akin. He was one of the incorporators of the Bank of Danville, which was chartered in 1818. He was also a contributor to the Danville Academy Fund, subscribing $250 between the years 1819 and 1823.

William Edwin Akin, a Second Lieutenant in Company D, 2nd Kentucky Regiment in 1846, served in the war with Mexico, and may have been the son of William, the silversmith.

According to the *Kentucky Reporter,* November 29, 1824, William Akin, merchant of Danville, died in Fredericktown, Maryland, in November, 1824.

ALRICH, JACOB N.

w. 1848—Louisville

The 1848 Louisville city directory lists Jacob N. Alrich as a "dealer in fancy goods" at 467 Market Street, between Third and Fourth. He was a member of the firm of J. N. Alrich and S. W. Warriner.

ALRICH, J. N., AND S. W. WARRINER

w. 1848—Louisville

This firm appeared in the 1848 Louisville city directory, although no address was given for them. It appears that J. N. Alrich was a jeweler, but S. W. Warriner was a silversmith. Mr. Warriner was living at the store in 1848.

AMOS, CORNELIUS

w. 1844-1856—Louisville

The early Louisville city directories do not use the same spelling in all issues for this silversmith's last name. The earliest directory in which he appears—1844-45—gives the spelling "Amos," but from that time on until 1856 the last name is spelled "Amiss." This may be due to the fact that many times names were spelled as they were pronounced. In 1844-45 and 1848 Cornelius Amos is listed as a silversmith; in 1848-49 he is listed as a watchmaker; in 1851-52 the directory lists him as a jeweler, while the 1855-56 directory lists no occupation for him. He was employed by E. C. Beard and Company. From 1844 until 1848 he was living on the north side of Walnut, later given the number of 340 Walnut, between Seventh and Eighth Streets. After that time he boarded at the home of Miss Ann Amiss.

ANDERSON, ANDREW

b. 1793

a. 1808-1814—Lexington

w. 1814-1844—Danville

Andrew Anderson served his apprenticeship under Asa Blanchard. In August, 1808, the Fayette County Court ordered: "Andrew Anderson, who will be fifteen years old in December next, be apprenticed to Asa Blanchard till he is twenty-one years old to learn the Silver and Goldsmith's trade, agreeable to law."

In 1844 the Danville and Houstonville Turnpike Road was incorporated, opening under the direction of an "A. Anderson," as well as others.

It would appear that after serving his apprenticeship under Blanchard in Lexington he practiced his profession in Danville.

ATKINSON, WILLIAM O.

w. 1848—Louisville

William O. Atkinson was employed at Henry Hudson's place of business, and he is listed as a silversmith in the 1848 Louisville city directory.

AYRES, EBENEZER BYRAM

c. 1816-1831

Ebenezer Byram Ayres, a silversmith, was in business at some time between 1816 and 1831. He was a brother of Elias Ayres, who was also a silversmith. It is not known where E. B. Ayres worked, although it is probable he followed his trade in Louisville.

AYRES, ELIAS

b. March 17, 1791—Morris Plains, New Jersey
d. January 5, 1842—Louisville
w. 1816-1831—Louisville

Elias Ayres was in partnership with Evans C. Beard. Although the date of the partnership's beginning is not known, on September 20, 1831, it was dissolved, and there is no further record of Elias Ayres as a silversmith. He was born March 17, 1791, at Morris Plains, New Jersey, the son of Silas Ayres and Mary Byram. He was a young man when he arrived in Louisville. He married Mary Ann Silliman of New Albany, Indiana, on July 27, 1819. His death occurred on January 5, 1842, and his will is recorded in the Jefferson County Will Book 4, page 281.

AYRES, E., AND COMPANY

w. 1816—Louisville

This firm of silversmiths was advertising in Louisville in 1816, and, according to *The Western Courier*, was located on Main Street.

AYRES AND BEARD

w. 1828-1831—Louisville

The partnership of Elias Ayres and Evans C. Beard was dissolved on September 20, 1831. Thomas Jefferson Shepard, from Georgetown, was employed by this firm from 1828 until 1831. How long the firm had been in business before employing Shepard is not known.

AYRES, SAMUEL

b. 1767—Essex County, Virginia
d. October 16, 1824—Danville
w. 1790-1823—Lexington
1823-1824—Danville

Samuel Ayres was born in Essex County, Virginia, in 1767. He came to the District of Kentucky in 1784, and by 1787 had settled in Lexington. Early in 1790 he advertised in *The Kentucky Gazette*:

> "SAMUEL AYRES
> Silver - Smith
> and
> J E W E L L E R
>
> Respectfully informs his friends and the Public, that he has lately opened a shop in Lexington, on Main street, nearly opposite Mr. Collin's Tavern; Ladies and Gentlemen, who honor him with their custom, may depend on having their commands complied with on the most reasonable terms, and on the shortest notice.
>
> JAN. 22, 1790."

In January, 1791, Samuel Ayres advertised: "WANTED, A quantity of old silver for which I will give five shillings per ounce."

In July, 1791, just a year and a half after opening his business in Lexington, he advertised: "SAMUEL AYRES. Silversmith and Jeweller.

Respectfully informs the public, that he has removed into the house he formerly lived in, on High Street, nearly opposite Mr. Kiser's tavern, where he intends carrying on his business in an extensive manner . . . ." Later in 1791 he advises his readers he is under obligation to start to the settlement on the 15th of December and asks those indebted to him, or having demands against him, to settle their accounts. He also advertises at this time for a sorrel colt, one year old, which had strayed about the 16th of October, and offers a reward of two dollars for his return.

Early in 1793 Samuel Ayres again advertised "Silversmith and Jeweler, has just returned to Lexington, and carries on the above business at his shop on Main Street two doors above Mr. M'Gowan's tavern . . . N.B. He will give one dollar per ounce for old silver."

The first printed directory for Lexington, published in 1806, lists Samuel Ayres as a silversmith on Main Street. He trained many apprentices in the art of silversmithing, and made a large quantity of very beautiful silver.

The Kentucky Gazette of February 28, 1795, carried Samuel Ayres' advertisement which read in part: ". . . removed his shop higher up on Main Street, next door above Mr. Moores and nearly opposite the Free Mason's Lodge." This was the corner of Main Street and Ayres Alley, where the Lafayette Hotel stands today. In 1795 his residence fronted Walnut Street.

Samuel Ayres and John G. Hiter entered into partnership June 3, 1813. Hiter had worked several years previously with skilled craftsmen in many parts of the country. It is not known how long this partnership endured, but in the 1818 Lexington city directory Mr. Ayres is listed on Main Street, and on April 21, 1819, *The Kentucky Gazette* carried the following advertisement: "Samuel Ayres informs Silversmiths, Merchants and others that he has lately established the manufacture of thimbles . . . also has for Sale Several Houses and Lots, also Tracts of Lands in this State and the State of Ohio."

In May, 1823, Samuel Ayres left Lexington, moving to Danville, where the business was carried on under the direction of his son, T. R. J. Ayres, until the Civil War.

When Mr. Ayres arrived in Danville in 1823, there were nine Baptists living within the city. Feeling it advisable that they establish a church, they met at one of the homes and organized the "First Baptist Church of Danville, Mercer [Boyle] County, Kentucky." Samuel Ayres and his wife, Dorothy, are the only names known of that original group of organizers.

Samuel Ayres died in Danville on October 16, 1824. The *Kentucky Reporter* of November 5, 1824, stated: "Departed this life after a short illness on the 16th ult, Mr. Samuel Ayres, in the 57th year of his age . . . Mr. Ayres was born in Essex County, Virginia, and emigrated to the state of Kentucky in 1784. . ."

The well preserved tombstone of Samuel Ayres, Sr., silversmith, is located southwest of the Dr. Ephraim McDowell Monument in the cemetery at Danville.

The Lexington Public Library owns some of the silversmith tools used by Samuel Ayres about 1830—a small anvil mounted on a section of a tree stump, a copper ladle and several anvils and raising hammers.

AYRES, THOMAS R. J.
w. 1823-1861—Danville

Thomas R. J. Ayres, silversmith, removed to Danville from Lexington with his father, Samuel Ayres, in 1823. A great deal of the silver yet to be found in the vicinity of Danville was made by T. R. J. Ayres. Samuel Ayres retired from the business upon moving to Danville, and the silversmith's trade was carried on by his son, T. R. J. Ayres, until the Civil War, when he moved from Danville to Iowa.

In 1833 T. R. J. Ayres and his brother, Dr. Samuel Ayres, moved into a building next to Hendren corner, which is reputed to be the oldest building on Main Street in Danville. The Ayres brothers purchased this building for $750 and received from Dr. Jefferson Polk only a quit-claim deed to the property. It is thought that the lot was at one time owned by John Warren, although no deed record has been found showing John Warren to have been the owner. There is no traceable deed for a period of nearly fifty years. Dr. Polk conveyed this property to the Ayres brothers, describing it in the deed as follows:

"And now is and has been for many years, in the occupancy of the said Thomas R. J. Ayres and Samuel Ayres as a silver shop."

It appears that the house was far from new when the Ayres brothers moved into it in 1833. Dr. Samuel Ayres remarked at the time he vacated the building in 1870 that he had been there "just thirty-seven years."

AYRES AND HITER
w. 1813—Lexington

On June 3, 1813, a partnership was formed between Samuel Ayres and John G. Hiter. Mr. Hiter had spent several years prior to this time working with skilled craftsmen in many parts of the country. The date of the partnership's dissolution is not known, but Samuel Ayres was advertising alone in 1819 and was listed alone in the 1818 Lexington city directory.

BAIRD, PLEASANT H.

w. 1813-1817—Paris

w. 1817-1838—Maysville

P. H. Baird began business in Paris, Kentucky, in 1813. He continued in the trade of silversmith and clockmaker in Paris until 1817 when he moved his business to Maysville. He served his apprenticeship under George Snyder and, in turn, had apprentices, as is shown by the record in the Mason County Deed Book N, which states that Strothers Reed was apprenticed to Pleasant H. Baird to learn "the trade and mystery of silversmith . . ." Both Reed and Baird were of Mason County.

In *The Kentucky Gazette* of June 4, 1811, is found the announcement of the marriage of Pleasant Baird of Lexington to Miss Mary McCall of Louisville.

From an advertisement in the *Maysville Eagle* we learn that P. H. Baird and Samuel Gulick were in the jewelry business in Maysville.

Mason County records show that P. H. Baird had a few real estate transactions. On April 3, 1814, lot No. 13 on Main Street in Washington, Kentucky, was deeded to James Frazer and Pleasant H. Baird by Henry Timberlake and Mary his wife, of Bourbon County, Kentucky. The price was $150, and the transaction is recorded in Deed Book N. Three years later, on March 25, 1817, Deed Book R, page 99, records a real estate transaction between James G. Arnold and Margaret, his wife, of Mason County, Kentucky, and Pleasant H. Baird of Mason County, "for $750 lot in Maysville, Mason County, Kentucky, fronting on Sutton street 30 ft. and running back 66 ft. adjoining the lot conveyed by Dr. L. A. McGhee to A. Crookshanks . . ." On March 8, 1831, Baird mortgaged the Maysville property to George Herbst for $500, and seven years later, on March 22, 1838, Pleasant H. Baird and his wife Mary "of Maysville, Kentucky," sold this parcel of ground to George Herbst for $2,000.

In the oldest cemetery in Maysville, just back of the Maysville Public Library, Sutton Street, their infant son is buried, the inscription on the marker reading: "Pleasant H. Baird, son of P. H. and Mary Baird, born 1-8-1819; killed 6-29-1824 by 'going on a tread mill'."

BARLOW, JAMES MADISON

b. July 9, 1812—Georgetown

w. 1835—Lexington

James Madison Barlow was born in Georgetown, Kentucky, on July 9, 1812. He, and his father and brothers, were to become famous for their many and varied inventions, among which were a cradling harvester, the Barlow knife, a locomotive, a cannon and an instrument used in the study of astronomy.

In 1835 J. M. Barlow was in Lexington. On May 27, 1835, the *Observer and Reporter* of that city carried a large advertisement wherein James M. Barlow advertises ". . . he is a silversmith and will make on short notice silver spoons, ladles, butter knives and sugar tongs."

James M. Barlow's wife, Elizabeth Barlow, was born in Scott County, Kentucky, the daughter of William Barlow who was born in Caroline County, Virginia, in 1767. James M. and Elizabeth Barlow had five children, namely: Bettie, born in Lexington (married H. Daniel); William, born in Lexington; Milt G., born in Lexington (married Mollie Muer); Thomas, born near Georgetown, died about 1837, age four years; Mary, born in Lexington (married R. H. Harkness).

J. M. Barlow's father, Thomas Barlow, was born August 25, 1760, and died on January 30, 1825. His mother was Susan Isbell, the daughter of James Isbell, a sea captain. J. M. Barlow's grandfather, Henry Barlow, was born in Caroline County, Virginia, in 1726 and died in 1814. Henry Barlow participated in the battle of Yorktown, October 1 to 18, 1781. He served under General LaFayette and witnessed the surrender of Lord Cornwallis and his combined British Army to the Republic commanded by General Washington.

J. M. Barlow's great-grandfather, Thomas Barlow, came to America from England about the year 1695.

BARNES, JAMES P.

w. 1848-1869—Louisville

Mr. Barnes, an Englishman of stocky build, was employed as a silversmith by William Kendrick, and he made a great deal of the silver sold by Mr. Kendrick during the time of his employment.

He advertised himself as a silversmith in Louisville in 1848-49. The 1851-52 Louisville city directory lists James P. Barnes, silversmith, living on the south side of Green, between Fourth and Fifth. He continued to be carried in the Louisville city directories until 1868-69.

In 1846 a James Barnes was a Sergeant in Company H of the First Regiment Kentucky Mounted Volunteers.

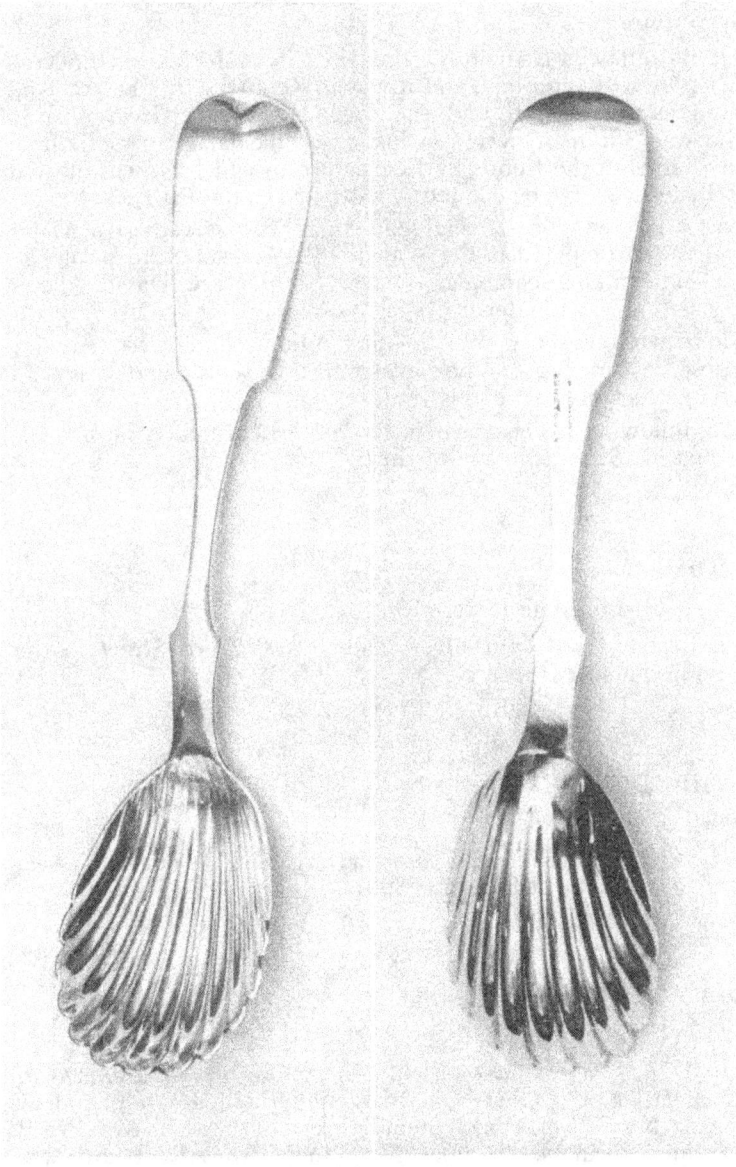

SILVER SHELL BOWL SPOON

Shell bowl, fiddle handle spoon with an unusual length of 7-17/32". Made by James P. Barnes, Louisville. Owned by Mr. and Mrs. John W. Luckett.

BARRETT, ROBERT

b. 1785—Virginia
d. 1821—Greensburg
w. Greensburg

Robert Barrett was born in Virginia in 1785. He arrived in Kentucky when he was yet a boy, and it was in Kentucky that he received his training as a silversmith and a jeweler. He lived in Green County where he was, for many years, a justice of the peace, served three successive terms in the Kentucky Legislature to which he was elected by the citizenry of Green County (1816, 1817 and 1818).

He was a strong, fine looking gentleman who served as a Major in the militia, participated in the War of 1812 as a subordinate officer, and in Gen. Hopkins' campaign he served in Capt. David Allen's Company as a First Lieutenant.

His shop in Greensburg was the first established in that city for the purpose of carrying on the silversmith's business, and it is said he was a "perfect master" of his trade.

In 1818, following his last year in the State Legislature, he became ill. He died in 1821 at the age of thirty-six.

BEAL, JOHN J.

w. 1845-1846—Louisville

John J. Beal is listed as a silver plater at 90 Third Street in the 1845-46 Louisville city directory.

BEAL, THEODORE L.

w. 1845-1846—Louisville

In the 1845-46 Louisville city directory we find Theodore L. Beal listed as a silver plater at 90 Third Street.

BEARD, EVANS C.

w. 1824-1875—Louisville

On July 5, 1824, William Kendrick, a lad of 14, was apprenticed to Evans C. Beard and continued learning under him for a period of seven years. No date has been found to establish when Mr. Beard first went into business. It does seem that Evans C. Beard was primarily a jeweler rather than a silversmith.

E. C. Beard was in partnership with Elias Ayres for a time. The date this partnership was formed is not known, but it was dissolved on September 20, 1831, and on that same date another partnership was announced, the new firm being comprised of E. C. Beard and George A. Zeumer. This new firm was known as E. C. Beard and Company. Their advertisement in the 1832 Louisville city directory listed silverplate, watches, clocks, music, pianofortes, percussion guns, pistol caps and lamps of every description offered for sale.

The 1838-39 Louisville directory listed Beard at 18 West Main and described his business as "jeweller and fancy store." At this time he lived on Jefferson between First and Second Streets. The city directories from 1841 through 1848-49 list Evans C. Beard with the firm of E. C. Beard and Company, while in 1851-52 he is listed alone as a jeweler, at "480 north side Main, between Fourth and Bullitt." The Louisville city directories continued to carry E. C. Beard until 1875.

BEARD AND AYRES

w. 1828-1831—Louisville

The date on which this partnership began operation is not known, however, Thomas Jefferson Shepard was employed by this firm in 1828 and continued working for them until the dissolution of the partnership on September 20, 1831. The two partners of this firm were Evans C. Beard and Elias Ayres.

BEARD, E. C., AND COMPANY

w. 1831-1852—Louisville

On September 20, 1831, the *Louisville Daily Journal* carried an advertisement which advised the public that Evans C. Beard was associated with George A. Zeumer under the firm name of E. C. Beard and Company.

The 1832 Louisville city directory lists E. C. Beard and Company, "fancy store," on the north side of Main between Fourth and Fifth Streets, where they continued for twenty-one years. The firm also had an advertisement in this directory which read:

"E. C. BEARD & CO., Wholesale and Retail
Watch and Clock, Fancy Jewelry, Military,
and Music Store
Louisville, Ky.
Piano Fortes, Percussion Guns and Pistols' Caps,
Silver Ware and Lamps, of every description,
constantly on hand."

From 1841 to 1849 E. C. Beard and Company were listed as jewelers, however, on page 122 of the 1844-45 Louisville city directory is an advertisement which reads in part—"Watch, Clock, Jewelry and Silver Smiths."

This firm employed Cornelius Amos from 1844 to 1852. William Kendrick was also employed by E. C. Beard and Company. When William Kendrick came to Louisville in 1824 he was soon working at E. C. Beard and Company as a jeweler's apprentice.

BEGGS, WILLIAM

w. 1841-1844—Louisville

William Beggs, silversmith, was employed at George Griffin's in Louisville from 1841 until 1844.

BENNETT, CHARLES FLETCHER

w. 1843-1848—Louisville

d. 1876—Louisville

The Louisville city directories list Charles Fletcher Bennett, silversmith, at Henry Fletcher's jewelry store from 1843 until 1848. In 1848 he was boarding at Ormsby House in Louisville.

Charles Fletcher Bennett was interred in Cave Hill Cemetery in Louisville on November 18, 1876.

BENNETT AND FLETCHER

w. 1830-1894—Louisville

The firm of Bennett and Fletcher advertised under many names in Louisville newspapers from 1830 to 1894. Among the names used were Henry Fletcher, Fletcher and Bennett, C. F. Bennett, C. Fletcher Bennett and Bennett, Fletcher and Company. The firm had a shop in Philadelphia as well as in Louisville. It seems reasonable to suppose that some of the silver sold in Louisville was made in Philadelphia, although silversmiths were employed by the Louisville store. Much of their silver is in existence today.

BENNETT, FLETCHER AND COMPANY

w. 1830-1894—Louisville

The advertising done by this firm, Bennett and Fletcher, and individuals connected with the firm over a long period of time makes it difficult to establish exact dates for any single company or individual.

However, between the Philadelphia company and the company operating in Louisville, a tremendous amount of silver of fine quality was made and sold. Much of this silver is still to be found in the possession of Kentucky families.

BERGANTZ, PETER W.

w. 1848-1852—Louisville

The 1848 Louisville city directory lists Peter W. Bergantz as a watch- and clockmaker on Fifth, between Market and Jefferson, however, the 1848-49 Directory lists Mr. Bergantz as a jeweler and carried his advertisement as such.

Shortly after 1849 Peter W. Bergantz became a partner in the firm of Bergantz and Frentz, and in the 1851-52 Louisville city directory he is shown with the firm of Bergantz and Frentz, and living at the same place. This firm employed Berg Christian, goldsmith, in 1851.

BEST, JOHN

1794—Shelby County
—Lexington

On January 25, 1794, John Best and Elizabeth Whitaker, daughter of Aquilla Whitaker, were married. The marriage is recorded in Shelby County's Marriage Record of 1792-1800. According to Mr. Charles R. Staples of Lexington, John Best went to Lexington, but the date of his arrival there is not known.

BLACKBURN, ————

w. 1812—Shelbyville

George L. Willis, Sr.'s *History of Shelby County, Kentucky*, published in 1929, lists a man named Blackburn as a silversmith in 1812. Diligent searching has unearthed nothing further concerning this silversmith of Shelbyville. There were many early citizens of Kentucky who bore the last name of Blackburn, and they accomplished many worthwhile things, but the information to be gleaned concerning them does not establish them as silversmiths.

BLANCHARD, ASA

w. 1818-1838—Lexington
d. September 15, 1838—Lexington

The name of Asa Blanchard has become more widely known than that of any other early silversmith of Kentucky, although making fine silver was not his only accomplishment. Some years ago Miss Mabel Weaks of Louisville copied the label as it appeared on a tall case clock in the Metropolitan Museum of Art which read:

> "Tall clock mahogany case with veneer of mahogany and inlay of satinwood. Probably made by Matthew Egerton, Jr., New Brunswick, N. J., early XIX cent. Works by A. Blanchard, Lexington, Ky. working about 1800-1810. Gift of George Coe Graves, 1930. The Sylmaris Coll."

The first definite date recorded for Blanchard is May 9, 1808, at which time the Fayette County Court awarded him an apprentice named William Grant, making it reasonable to assume that he was making silver for some time prior to this date. The 1818 Lexington city directory lists Asa Blanchard, "Gold and Silver Smith, Mill and Short streets."

Asa Blanchard had many apprentices. The following bond, quoted in part, illustrates the rigid discipline required of an apprentice, as well as the silversmith's responsibility. The Fayette County Deed Book 1, page 418, records the bond of Simon Bradford to Asa Blanchard:

> "August 9, 1814. Simon Bradford, son of Fielding Bradford, of Scott County, voluntarily apprentices himself to Asa Blanchard of the Town of Lexington, to learn the art, trade and mistery of a Silver Smith and after the manner of an apprentice to serve him faithfully until he arrives at the age of 21 years, which will be on September 6, 1818, all of which time he, the said apprentice, his master shall faithfully serve, his secrets keep, his lawful commands everywhere obey. He shall do no damage to his master nor see it done by others, without telling or giving notice thereof to his said master. He shall not waste his master's goods nor lend them unlawfully to others with his own goods or the goods of others. He shall neither buy or sell without license from his said master. He shall not commit Fornication nor contract matrimony during the said term. At cards, dice, or any other unlawful game he shall not play whereby his master may sustain damage. He shall not absent himself day or night from his said master's service without his leave, nor haunt alehouses, Taverns or play-houses during the said term but in all things behave himself as a faithful apprentice ought to do during the said term, and the said Asa Blanchard . . . agrees to find the said apprentice good and sufficient boarding, washing and lodging . . . during the full term of his apprenticeship and . . . shall use the utmost of his endeavors to teach or cause him to be taught the art, trade or mistery of a Silver Smith and agrees to pay the said Simon Bradford $50 at the expiration of the third year of his apprenticeship, the said apprentice is to furnish his cloathing.
> F. BRADFORD   SIMON BRADFORD   ASA BLANCHARD"

In August of 1808, a few months after Blanchard was awarded Simon Bradford as an apprentice, Andrew (Alex) Anderson was apprenticed to Blanchard. Andrew Anderson was just under fifteen years of age at the time he began his apprenticeship, and served until he was twenty-one years old. James I. Lemon moved to Lexington

RARE BLANCHARD LADLES

Top: Ladle owned by J. Winston Coleman, Jr., engraved initial "C", formerly owned by his grandfather, David S. Coleman.
Bottom: Ladle owned by William H. Townsend, engraved initial "T", formerly owned by Abraham Lincoln's father-in-law, Robert S. Todd.

from Scott County to learn the trade under Asa Blanchard. Eli Garner was another Blanchard apprentice, as was George Easley. Blanchard's will left his tools to Easley and Garner, with the request they enter into partnership, but his request was disregarded. Easley disappeared from Lexington, and Garner became a partner in the firm of Garner and Winchester.

During the thirty years he was in business in Lexington Asa Blanchard used a variety of marks. Probably no other silversmith in Kentucky used as many during his years as a craftsman. Blanchard has been considered the maker of some silver which was marked simply "A.B." The authors have never seen a proven piece of Blanchard silver with this stamp.

In 1911 the Frankfort Presbyterian Church, Frankfort, Kentucky, lent three Blanchard mugs to be used in an exhibit at The Metropolitan Museum of Art, which exhibit was composed of silver used in New York, New Jersey and the South. Item 19 in that exhibit was a mug six inches high, marked "A. BLANCHARD" in a long oval. Item 20 was two mugs, each 4¼ inches high, marked in the same manner. All of the mugs were inscribed "Frankfort Presbyterian Church."

Blanchard made many of the silver cups given as premiums at the early fairs, as well as items ordered for household use. Three silver cups made by Blanchard are owned by The Filson Club in Louisville and bear the inscription "K.A. PREMIUM." Blanchard's customers included some of Kentucky's most prominent personages. He made a teapot for Isaac Shelby, Kentucky's first governor, plus a very beautiful pair of candlesticks with the initials of Isaac Shelby on one candlestick, and the initials of his wife on the other. Before 1819 Blanchard made a silver tea service for General Green Clay, and the silver service which Henry Clay gave his wife was also made by Blanchard.

Matthew H. Jouett, a renowned portrait painter of Kentucky's early days, painted portraits of both Asa Blanchard and his first wife, Rebecca.

Blanchard advertised in *The Kentucky Gazette* of August 28, 1818: "Gold and Silver patent lever Watches. Keeps constantly on hand a large assortment of SILVER WARE warranted of the best kind such as COFFEE AND TEA POTS, SLOP BOWLS, SUGAR DISHES, CREAM EWERS, PITCHERS, CANNS, TUMBLERS, LADLES AND SPOONS OF ALL KINDS . . . ."

On June 30, 1809, Blanchard purchased from Samuel Wilkinson a lot on Mill Street, and on August 14, 1810, he purchased from Elder Matthew an additional lot at the corner of Mill and Short Streets. This was the location in which he began his business career in Lexington, and here he carried on his business until his death in 1838.

The estate of Asa Blanchard was a sizable one, amounting to nearly $40,000, made up of stocks, shares, notes, cash and property. He did not claim any interest in the estate of his second wife, this provision having been covered in their marriage contract. Robert Frazer, Jr., another silversmith of Kentucky's early days, was one of the estate appraisers.

The date of Asa Blanchard's birth is not known, but the *Lexington Observer & Reporter* of September 19, 1838, advised that Asa Blanchard, of Lexington, died September 15, 1838, at an advanced age. *The Kentucky Gazette* of September 20, 1838, read—"DIED—on 15th inst., Asa Blanchard, of Lexington, an old and worthy citizen." His first wife, Rebecca, died after 1827. On March 7, 1838, Asa Blanchard remarried. His second wife, Mrs. Hester Harris, was a widow of some means. Mr. Blanchard passed away six months and eight days after his marriage to Mrs. Harris. He had two children by his first marriage, a daughter—Mary L., who was married, May 8, 1828, to Charles S. Gatewood, and a son—Horace F., who lived but a few months after his father's death.

BORDERSEN, CHRISTIAN

w. 1850—Russellville

Christian Bordersen was working in Russellville in 1850.

BRADFORD, SIMON

b. September 6, 1797

w. 1814-1819—Lexington

Simon Bradford was awarded to Asa Blanchard as an apprentice on August 9, 1814. Bradford was twenty-one years of age on September 6, 1818, and on his twenty-first birthday had completed his apprenticeship. He spent but a short time practicing his profession, as is shown by the fact that he sold all of his stock in 1819.

BRIGAM, THOMAS

w. 1832—Louisville

The 1832 Louisville city directory lists Thomas Brigam, a silver plater. He worked on Third Street between Main and Market.

BROOKWAY AND BACON

w. 1836—Louisville

The Louisville city directory for 1836 lists this firm as jewelers, whose place of business was located on the south side of Main Street, between Sixth and Seventh Streets.

BRYANT, BUTLER

w. 1838-1848—Louisville

Butler Bryant was a silversmith who worked in Louisville for at least ten years. The Louisville city directories for 1838-39 and 1843-44 show he was working for the firm of W. & A. Cooper during this time. From 1844 to 1848 he was apparently in business for himself. In 1844 he was located on the north side of Grayson, between Jackson and Hancock. In 1845 his place of business was at 467 Market and he was living near his shop at 543 Market, where he still resided in 1848.

BRYSON, EDWARD A.

w. 1841-1848—Louisville

Edward A. Bryson is listed in the Louisville city directories as an engraver from 1841 to 1845, with his place of business on the west side of Wall Street near Main. It would appear that engraving was Mr. Bryson's own particular accomplishment, although he also sold silver made at his shop. In the 1843-44 Louisville city directory we find a George H. Forsyth, silversmith, working at E. A. Bryson's.

In 1848 "Edward A." Bryson is not listed, but an "Edmund A." Bryson, engraver, is. It is possible that the difference in the spelling of the first name was an error made in the preparation of the directory.

BURKE, EDMUND K.

w. 1841—Louisville

Edmund K. Burke was a jeweler. He was employed by George Griffin in 1841. George Griffin was a Louisville manufacturer of silver articles.

BURNETT, B. L.

w.   -1857—Lexington

B. L. Burnett was a manufacturer of silverware. In 1857 he ceased manufacturing silver articles due to the difficulties created by competition in the East. His reasons for closing his business at this time would tend to indicate that he had been engaged in this business for some years. It was about this time that new methods of manufacture brought to a close the era of "hand-wrought" silver by the craftsmen.

BUSH, PHILIP, JR.

b. February 22, 1765

d. January, 1807—Frankfort

Philip Bush, Jr. was born in Winchester, Virginia, February 22, 1765, the son of Philip Bush and Catherine Slough Bush. His parents moved to Virginia from Mannheim, Germany, about 1750.

On July 10, 1787, Philip Bush, Jr., advertised himself in Winchester, Virginia, as a "jeweler and goldsmith at the Golden Urn, ..." He made a great deal of silver, including small items in both gold and silver. However, the following year he advertised his lease for sale.

On April 28, 1794, a Winchester, Virginia, newspaper carried his advertisement for a shoemaker (preferably a single man) "as he was wanted to go to Kentucky." He arrived in Kentucky about the turn of the century. On November 1, 1806, *The Western World* of Frankfort, Kentucky, announced—"PHIL BUSH'S TAVERN, FRANKFORT (Where the Farmer's Bank now is) Washington Inn—the spacious additional buildings commenced last Spring are in such a state of forwardness as to enable him to accommodate any number of gentlemen that may please to call on him. His lodging rooms are commodious and well furnished with bedding equal to any in this State. His stable large and finished in a style equal to any in the U. S. and well furnished with corn, oats and hay. From the long experience he has had in that line of business he flatters himself that he will give general satisfaction.—PHIL BUSH."

Mr. Bush's father was a widely known tavern keeper, and his son, Philip, Jr., must have had much experience in the business. No information has been found to indicate that Philip Bush, Jr., ever made silver after coming to Kentucky. Philip Bush was listed as a taxpayer in Fayette County, Kentucky, as early as 1790. This could have been the silversmith or his father, although neither of them was living in Kentucky at that time.

On January 15, 1807, *The Western World* of Frankfort, Kentucky, contained this notice:

"PHIL BUSH dead, but Mrs. Bush will run Washington Inn."

BYRNE, JOHN
c. 1846-1859—Lexington

John Byrne was born in Ireland. He came to Lexington about 1846, and the 1859 Lexington city directory lists him as a silver plater. He invented a stone-cutting machine and shortly thereafter left the business of silversmithing.

CACHOT, FELIX FERJEUX
w. 1813-1839—Bardstown
d. 1839—Bardstown

Felix F. Cachot was one of Kentucky's most colorful silversmiths of the early nineteenth century. He was a Frenchman who, with other Trappist Monks under the supervision of Father Urban, fled France during the Jacobin War in 1803. They first sought refuge in

Silversmiths of Kentucky

the Holy Valley in Switzerland, then during the winter of 1803-1804, the group came to America. For a few years they located at Monk's Mound, Illinois. By 1813 Father Urban was so discouraged he decided to return to France. He released from their vows those who so desired it, that they might remain in America and pursue the trades in which they had been trained.

Three of the men remained in America, Ignatius Hottenroth, Felix F. Cachot and Peter Goetes, who made their perilous way to Bardstown in Nelson County. Cachot's shop was located next to what is now known as 212 E. Stephen Foster Avenue in Bardstown. He was an excellent silversmith and jeweler as well as a clock- and watchmaker. His engraving was beautifully done in a small, ornamented French script.

Hottenroth was drowned in 1817 and the Nelson County Order Book of 1817 shows that Cachot was appointed the administrator of John Ignatius Hottenroth's estate, which required a $5,000 bond and the appointment of appraisers.

Following the death of Hottenroth, Cachot made his will, which was executed July 28, 1817. This worn and faded document, now one hundred and thirty-six years old, is in the Nelson County court house in Bardstown. The will reproduced here was copied from the Nelson County Will Book H, page 557:

"In the name of God Amen. I FELIX F. CASHOT of Nelson County in the State of Kentucky being at the present time in my usual health and strength of mind but knowing that all men are mortal and bond to die do make this my last Will and Testament. My soul I return to Almighty God the Giver of it and my body to the dust of the earth from whence it came as to Worldly Goods it has pleased God to help me to. I give and bequeath them as follows, to wit, my debts first to be paid By my executors herein named—One hundred dollars to be immediately given for the Benefit of the holy Roman Cholock church—For the relief of his soul suffering in the flames of Purgatory.—I then will and wish that Peter M. Gates who now lives with me to be the sole legatee to all the Ballance of my Estate both real and personal after this my will is put in Execution *and at the end of the said year* to be accountable to the Roman Chatholic church for the purpose of praying for the souls departed for one half of the money part the real Estate to be his forever and the other half to be the sole property of the said Peter M. Gates to do as he pleases with I hereby nominate and appoint the said Peter M. Gates Executor to this my last Will and Testament hereby revoking all former Wills either written or verbal made by me— In Testimony whereof I the said Felix F. Cashot have hereunto set my hand and affixed my seal this 28th day of July in the year of our Lord and Saviour one thousand eight hundred and seventeen.

Felix F. Cashot (Seal)

Witness, present
    A. Hubbard
    Thomas Howard
    Jacob Sowhey

The slaves to be free after my debts is paid. Ann is to be set at Liberty by paying Peter M. Gates $150.00 out of my property, William *his* to be free at and Little Black Peter, at the same time. They must be bound to a trade to Mr. Peter M. Gates or other

F. F. Cashot

At the last survivor of the two that is the last of us both Cashot and Gates to set them two Boys William and Peter free at his death in his Will.

F. F. Cashot

1833 July 23 in addition to my Will and Testament. This few lines I have added in a hurry to my last will which I hope will be admitted.

F. F. Cashot"

His will was probated September 9, 1839.

Peter M. Gates referred to in the will was the same Peter Goetes who had arrived in Bardstown with Cachot. The codicil to the originally prepared will, added sixteen years later, was done in Cachot's own handwriting as was the original will prepared in 1817. The spelling and punctuation were his own. Felix F. Cachot did not continue to spell his name "Cachot," but changed it to "Cashot," probably because of the local pronunciation given it.

CASWELL, SAMUEL

w. 1838-1846—Louisville

Samuel Caswell was a silversmith and watchmaker. He was employed at S. Hockersmith's in 1838 and at George Griffin's in 1843, according to the Louisville city directories. He was listed alone as a watchmaker in 1841, and as a silversmith in 1845-46. He was interred in Cave Hill Cemetery in Louisville on April 20, 1878.

CHAPEL, H.

w. 1845-1846—Louisville

H. Chapel was a silver plater working at 597 Main Street in Louisville. He appeared in the Louisville city directory only once.

CHOATE, STEPHEN D.

w. 1841-1852—Louisville

Stephen D. Choate was a gold- and silversmith. In 1841 he was located on the south side of Jefferson between Brook and Floyd. By 1845 his shop was at 493 Main, and he was living at 61 First Street, between Green and Walnut Streets. By 1848 he was located on Fourth between Main and Market Streets. Later that year he had moved again, this time to Fifth between Main and Market Streets. The 1848-49 Louisville city directory lists him under the heading of "Silver and Gold Smiths." The 1851-52 directory places him as a "Jewelry, Gold and Silver Smith" at "99 south side of Fourth, between Main and Market."

CHRISTY, THOMAS

w. 1794—Lexington

Thomas Christy arrived in Lexington in 1794. During the month of April and the first part of May, 1794, *The Kentucky Gazette* carried the following advertisement for him:

"THOMAS CHRISTY,
Gold Smith and Jeweller

RESPECTFULLY informs the public in general, that he has just commenced business in Lexington, on Main street, opposite Dr. Downing's, where he carries on the Gold, Silver and Plating business, in all their various branches — Devices in hair, and miniature Painting—Mourning Rings and Lockets of every description for Ladies, as elegant as those imported from Europe, or manufactured in any part of the United States—Ladies and Gentlemen who will please to favor him with their custom, shall have their work done on the shortest notice, and on the most moderate terms."

How long he remained in Lexington is not known. No further information concerning him was found.

CONERY, A.

w. 1838-1854—Frankfort

A. Conery was the owner of a jewelry store in Frankfort. In 1838 and 1839 W. P. Loomis advertised in *The Commonwealth* of Frankfort "Watch and Clock repairing at Mr. Conery's Jewelry Store." In the years that followed, Mr. Conery and W. P. Loomis were in business together, Mr. Conery being Mr. Loomis' assistant. When Mr. Loomis became unable to continue the management of his business because of advanced age, Mr. Conery managed the store until Mr. Loomis' death, at which time the business was closed. Their establishment was located on Main Street in Frankfort.

COOPER, ARCHABALD

w. 1841-1848—Louisville

w. 1842-   —Frankfort

Archabald Cooper was a silversmith. He first appears in the 1841 Louisville city directory, and was a partner in the firm of W. & A. Cooper. In 1841 A. Cooper was living on the south side of Green

Street between Second and Third Streets. In 1848 he was boarding at Bowles' house. The firm of W. & A. Cooper opened a shop in Frankfort in February, 1842.

COOPER, WILLIAM

w. 1841-1844—Louisville
w. 1842-   —Frankfort

William Cooper was a silversmith and a member of the partnership of W. & A. Cooper. The 1841 Louisville city directory shows William Cooper with the firm of W. & A. Cooper. At this time he lived on the south side of Green between Second and Third Streets with his partner, Archabald Cooper. In 1843-44 the directory advises that his place of business was on the east side of Third, between Main and Water Streets, and he was living at the Exchange Hotel. In February of 1842 the firm of W. & A. Cooper opened a shop in Frankfort.

COOPER, WILLIAM & ARCHABALD

w. 1838-1841—Louisville
w. 1842-   —Frankfort

This very excellent firm of silversmiths appeared in the Louisville city directories from 1838 through 1841. Both members of the firm were silversmiths in their own right, and they employed other silversmiths as well. From 1838 until 1848 Butler Bryant, a silversmith, was working for this company, as was James C. Fulton, a watchmaker, in 1841, and Daniel F. Winchester, another silversmith, in 1841. Their shop in Louisville was located at 72 West Main Street in 1838 and 1839, but two years later they were on the west side of Fourth Street, between Main and Market.

On February 11, 1842, *The Commonwealth* of Frankfort carried the following announcement for this firm:

> "W. & A. COOPER, Manufacturers of all kinds of SILVER WARE, and Dealers in Jewelry, Fancy Goods, Brittania Ware and Cutlery, having opened a house in Frankfort, they offer for sale a great variety of the above named articles, of the most recent importations, all of which they will sell at the most reduced prices.
>
> They have also some fine specimens of their SILVER WORK AND DRAWINGS.
>
> They will be pleased to exhibit to those who may favor them with a call.
>
> They have taken a Store on Main Street, next door to Mr. Vest's residence.
>
> Frankfort, January 12, 1842"

CRAB, JARED
w. 1823—Elkton

Jared Crab was an early craftsman who worked in Todd County about 1823.

CUNNINGHAM, ROBERT
w. 1844-1845—Louisville

Robert Cunningham, a silversmith, was working in Louisville on Gray Street, between Jackson and Hancock, during 1844 and 1845.

CURTIS, D.
w. 1820—Lexington

D. Curtis arrived in Lexington in 1820. How long he remained there is problematical, for he does not appear in any of the city directories. On June 21, 1820, the *Kentucky Reporter* carried a report of a big fire on the night of June 14th. Eight stores on West Main Street were destroyed, including that of D. Curtis, silversmith, who lost everything.

DAUMON, E. J., AND COMPANY
w. 1820—Lexington

This firm was advertising in Lexington in 1820.

DAUMONT, PETER
w. 1843-1846—Louisville

Peter Daumont was a jeweler. From 1843 until early in 1845 he was employed by R. E. Smith. The 1845-46 Louisville city directory lists him alone, with his place of business at 46 First Street.

DeYOUNG, ELIAS, AND COMPANY
w. 1836-1839—Louisville

This firm advertised in the 1836 Louisville city directory:

"E. DeYOUNG & CO., Jewelry and Fancy Store, Fourth cross st., between Main and Market streets.

Keeps always on hand a fine assortment of Jewelry and Fancy Goods, Wholesale and Retail. N.B. All kinds of Jewelry, Watches, combs, etc., repaired with neatness and dispatch."

The company's place of business in 1836 was on the east side of Fourth Street, between Main and Market, but by 1838 they were on the north side of Main, between Floyd and Preston.

DICKSON, HENRY
b. 1774
d. 1854
w. Paintsville

Henry Dickson, silversmith, was a man of many talents, all of which served his community well. He was born in 1774. He married Joyce Farmer, who bore him four children—three boys and one girl.

The Floyd County Tax List of October 4, 1837, shows him to have been a property owner. He lived in the eastern section of Kentucky, where the town of Paintsville was later established. Henry Dickson prepared the plans for the town and on February 24, 1834, the act establishing Paintsville was approved.

He owned a grist mill on Paint Creek. He was also a Baptist minister who was a motivating force for good in the community. His services were well attended, due in part, perhaps, to the fact that he always took his fiddle to service and opened and closed the service by playing several numbers.

Henry Dickson and his brother came to Kentucky from Grayson County, Virginia, in 1814. For nearly fifty years they were leaders in their community, owned large tracts of land and were prosperous people.

This silversmith made many silver pins and brooches, one of which was worn for many years by Mrs. Susan J. Connelly, a pioneer of eastern Kentucky.

DOLFINGER, JACOB
b. July 26, 1820
d. May, 1892
w. 1848-1861—Louisville

Jacob Dolfinger was a gold- and silversmith. He was born on July 26, 1820, in Weildiestadt, Wuertenberg, Germany. In 1847 he arrived in Louisville, where he worked seven years for Henry Hudson. He opened his own place of business at 113 Fourth Street in 1858. Here he manufactured silverware, jewelry, and like products. From 1859 to 1861 he was a member of the firm of Hirschbuhl and Dolfinger in Louisville.

In 1855 Jacob Dolfinger and Henry Hudson entered into partnership. This arrangement lasted less than two years.

It has not been learned when Jacob Dolfinger left Louisville, but in May of 1892 he died at the home of his eldest daughter in Weisbaden, Germany.

DORSEY, HENRY C.

w. 1845-1846—Louisville

Henry C. Dorsey, a silversmith, was working in Louisville in 1845 and 1846. He resided at 495 Green Street.

DRAPER, JOSEPH

w. 1825-1832—Wilmington, Delaware
w. 1849-   —Cincinnati, Ohio
w.   —Hopkinsville

Joseph Draper was indeed a silversmith. Whether he worked in the State of Kentucky is problematical. On February 3, 1832, he advertised in the *Delaware Journal:* "Silversmith—The subscriber, intending to leave the State, . . . Joseph Draper, Silversmith and Jeweler."

One source places him in Cincinnati in 1849 and in Hopkinsville, Kentucky, at an undetermined date.

DUMESNILL, ANTHONY

w. 1818-1833—Lexington
d. 1833

Anthony Dumesnill was a silversmith and watchmaker. The Lexington city directory for 1818 lists him as a watchmaker and a jeweler, with his place of business on Mill Street. He and his wife both died of cholera in 1833.

DUMONT, P.

w. 1844-1846—Louisville

P. Dumont worked in Louisville. His jewelry shop was located at 493 Main Street, and he lived on the west side of First Street between Green and Walnut. In the city directories for 1844-45 and 1845-46 he is carried as a "jeweller."

DUNCAN, WILLIAM HENRY
Prior to 1850

Very little information has been found concerning William Henry Duncan other than the fact he worked in Kentucky prior to 1850. One source of information places him in Washington County, and another gives Springfield as his place of residence. A William Duncan is on the Shelby County Tax List for 1792-1795.

EASLEY, GEORGE
w. 1838—Lexington

George Easley is listed in the 1838-39 Lexington city directory as a silversmith, boarding at Asa Blanchard's. He was apprenticed to Blanchard and apparently found favor with the master craftsman, for when Blanchard died in 1838 his will made provision for his tools to be given to George Easley and Eli Garner, another Blanchard apprentice. Mr. Blanchard also expressed the wish that these two silversmiths enter into a business partnership, but his request was not fulfilled. George Easley soon disappeared from Lexington, and no further record is found concerning him.

EAVES, W., AND A. FALIZE
w. 1842—Lexington

The *Observer and Reporter*, on April 20, 1842, carried this firm's advertisement in which they advised they "have opened shop on West Main where they will manufacture all kinds of jewelry, silverware, and do engraving."

ELDER, EDWARD
c. 1812—Lexington

L. L. Tod prepared from memory a list of the men who were on the roll of the Lexington Light Infantry under the command of Captain Nathaniel G. Hart, during the War of 1812. One of the men listed was "Edw. Elder, Silversmith."

ERENS, JOHN
w. 1845-1846—Louisville

John Erens was a goldsmith, who worked in Louisville at 53 Seventh Street.

ERWIN, THOMAS M.

w. 1845-1846—Louisville

d. February, 1889—Louisville

In 1845 and 1846 Thomas M. Erwin, silversmith, was working in Louisville. He resided at 503 Green Street. Captain Thomas M. Erwin was interred in Cave Hill Cemetery in Louisville on February 17, 1889.

ESTERLE, JACOB R.

b. 1814—France

d. January 30, 1868—Louisville

w. 1835-1868—Louisville

Jacob R. Esterle was born in France in 1814. He, together with Joseph Werne, came to America, and settled in Louisville sometime between 1832 and 1835. He worked as a silversmith and watchmaker until the time of his death in 1868.

ETHRIDGE, JOHN E.

w. 1838-1848—Louisville

d. December, 1894—Louisville

The Louisville city directories from 1838 to 1848 list John Ethridge as a silver plater. His place of business was located on Market between Seventh and Eighth Streets. He died in 1894 and was interred in Cave Hill Cemetery, Louisville, on December 6, 1894.

EUBANK AND JEFFRIES

c. 1820-1834—Glasgow

This firm of silversmiths succeeded William Savage in business. The partnership was later dissolved, and each man then established his own business.

EUBANK, JAMES

c. 1816-1855—Glasgow

James Eubank, silversmith, came to Kentucky from Virginia. James and his brother, Joseph, were in partnership until about 1841. Following the dissolution of their partnership, each brother opened his own shop.

The Barren County Marriage Records show that James Eubank married Mary Bransford in 1833. Random notes from suits, filed in the office of the Bourbon County Circuit Clerk (Samuel Givens' Hrs. vs. James Eubank, Box 479, Dec. 3, 1816), records:

> "Samuel Lamme and Samuel Givens sold to James Eubank a tract in Washington County, Kentucky on waters of Panther's Creek. Hrs. listed in suit under date of Nov. 9, 1819; William Craig and Margaret, his wife, late Givens; John Givens; James Givens; George Givens; Patsy Givens; Isabella, Elizabeth, Ann, and Jane Givens, four last being infants under 21 years, by James Givens, their guardian, hrs. of Samuel Givens, decd."

EUBANK, JOSEPH

c. 1829-1855—Glasgow

Joseph Eubank, silversmith, and his brother, James Eubank, came to Kentucky from Virginia, and were in partnership until about 1841, after which time they operated separate shops.

Joseph Eubank and Elizabeth McMillin were married in 1829 in Glasgow.

EUBANK, JAMES AND JOSEPH

w. 1834-1841—Glasgow

James and Joseph Eubank, silversmiths, were brothers who came to Kentucky from Virginia. They succeeded William Savage in business and operated in partnership until 1841, when the partnership was dissolved, and each of the brothers established his own shop. A great deal of the silver made by these men is marked "J & J EUBANK" "GLASGOW."

EWING, WARREN B.

c. 1840-1876—Shelbyville

Warren B. Ewing was a very excellent silversmith. He was born in Bourbon County, where he spent the early years of his life. In the early 1840's he came to Shelbyville where he worked for his brother-in-law, J. S. Sharrard, an established silversmith, and with whom he resided.

Aside from his accomplishments as a silversmith, Warren B. Ewing was a well educated man, played the flute and was an accomplished violinist. The *Shelby County Record* of October 12, 1917, says in part: "That he was disappointed in love and just threw himself away is evidenced by a poem, written by himself, just twenty years before his death."

FLAIG, EDWARD

c. 1830—Danville

Spoons bearing the name of Edward Flaig are known. On West Walnut Street in Danville is a house well over one hundred years old, which has been known for many years as the "Flaig House." In years gone by it was the home of Judge Thomas P. Young, who was the father of Mrs. Edward Flaig.

FLETCHER, HENRY

w. 1818-1830—Lexington
w. 1830-1866—Louisville
d. 1866—Louisville

Henry Fletcher, jeweler, was listed in the 1818 Lexington city directory, and was advertising in Lexington as early as 1818 and 1819. His shop was on the south side of Main, between Fourth and Fifth Streets. He moved from Lexington to Louisville in 1830, where he continued in business for many years.

On November 24, 1830, the *Louisville Daily Journal* carried Henry Fletcher's advertisement which advised the public of the opening of his business on Main Street. He solicited orders for sets of silver plate, which would be executed in Philadelphia. Henry Fletcher had a very comprehensive, full page advertisement in the 1845-46 Louisville city directory. He advertised "Wholesale and Retail Dealer in Clocks, Watches, Jewelry, Silverware, Military Goods, Lamps, Etc., No. 463 Main, between 4th and 5th," and enumerated gold and silver watches, jewelry, silver spoons, forks and butter knives, castors, candlesticks, razors, spectacles, walking sticks, watchmakers tools and materials, etc., as well as "Silver Plate Spoons, Forks, etc., manufactured to order."

Henry Fletcher employed many skilled craftsmen. From 1832 until at least 1838 Henry Fletcher employed Abner Reeves, a watchmaker. During 1838 and 1839 Francis A. Griswold, another watchmaker, was employed by him, while in 1843 and 1844 we find Charles F. Bennett, a silversmith, working for Fletcher. From 1841 to 1849 John J. Klink, a jeweler and watchmaker, was employed at Henry Fletcher's.

Henry Fletcher's active and successful business career ended in 1866. On July 15, 1866, he was interred in Cave Hill Cemetery, Louisville.

FLETCHER AND BENNETT

w. 1830-1894—Louisville and Philadelphia

Shops were maintained by this firm in both Louisville and Philadelphia. Much of the silver sold in Louisville was actually made in Philadelphia, for they advertised that orders would be executed in Philadelphia. They also employed silversmiths, watchmakers, etc., in Louisville, which would indicate that a part of the silver they sold was made in Louisville. During the long and active life of this firm they advertised in varying ways: C. F. Bennett, C. Fletcher Bennett, Bennett, Fletcher and Company, Henry Fletcher, and Fletcher and Bennett.

FORSYTH, GEORGE H.

w. 1843-1848—Louisville

George H. Forsyth, a silversmith, was employed at E. A. Bryson's in 1843. At this time he lived on Brook, between Market and Jefferson Streets. In 1848 he was listed in the Louisville city directory as a silversmith working at 62 Fourth Street. He lived first, in 1844, on Brook between Market and Jefferson Streets. In 1845 he was living at 220 Fifth, while in 1848 he was living at 109 Fifth, between Market and Jefferson Streets.

FOSTER, JEREMIAH

b. 1791

d. 1823—Christian County

w. Hopkinsville

Jeremiah Foster was Christian County's first silversmith. He was born in 1791 and died in 1823 at the age of thirty-two. He was buried in the old Baptist (or Pioneer) graveyard, and his will is recorded in the Christian County Court records.

FRAZER, ALEXANDER

b. Ireland

d. November 7, 1810—Lexington

w. -1799—Paris

w. 1800-1810—Lexington

Alexander Frazer, silversmith, came to America from Ireland. His brother, Robert Frazer, was also a silversmith. The two brothers were in Philadelphia for a while, then came to Kentucky, settling in Paris where they were in business with Thomas Phillips of that city. Their business included clock- and watchmaking as well as jewelry and silversmithing. Their partnership with Thomas Phillips was dissolved on March 26, 1799. Robert went to Lexington, followed shortly by Alexander. Apparently they were both established in Lexington sometime during 1800. Lexington's first printed directory, published in 1806, lists Alexander Frazer as a silversmith.

Alexander Frazer married Miss Nancy Oliver of Jessamine County on December 20, 1804. They had two sons—James, the eldest who died when still a young man, and Oliver, who became the well-known portrait painter.

He supported his family well, but before he could make adequate provision for their future, he died. *The Kentucky Gazette,* on November 13, 1810, read: "Alexander Frazer, a native of Ireland, but for several years a resident of Lexington, Kentucky. Died November 7, 1810." Less than six years after his marriage, and shortly after the birth of his second son, Alexander's wife, Nancy, was left with the problem of supporting and educating their two sons.

Alexander's bachelor brother, Robert, voluntarily accepted the responsibility of educating James and Oliver. He placed them in Lexington's best school and later financed Oliver's sojourn abroad where he studied for several years.

FRAZER, ROBERT

    b. 1769—Ireland
    d. 1851—Lexington
    w. 1799—Paris
    w. 1799-1851—Lexington

Robert Frazer, an outstanding man and a very successful silversmith, was born in Ireland in 1769. He and his brother, Alexander, came to America and went first to Philadelphia. Later they moved to Kentucky, where they settled in Paris. They were in partnership with Thomas Phillips in Paris until March 26, 1799, when the partnership was dissolved. Following the dissolution of the business partnership in Paris, Robert Frazer went to Lexington that same year and his brother, Alexander, followed not too long after.

Robert Frazer opened his shop in Lexington on Main Street opposite the Court House. On August 10, 1801, he advertised he had "moved to the house lately occupied by Stewart's printing office, opposite to Brent's tavern, where he will continue in the watchmaking and silversmiths trade." The first printed directory of Lexington, published in 1806, lists Robert Frazer, silversmith.

When Robert Frazer's brother, Alexander, died in 1810, leaving a widow and two sons, Robert assumed the financial responsibility of the children's education. Both boys were placed in Lexington's finest school. James, the eldest nephew, died when but a young man. Oliver Frazer was sent abroad to study for several years, and became a very well known portrait painter.

Robert Frazer had a famous guest in 1846. Louis Phillipe, King of France, had commissioned George P. R. Healey, portrait painter, to paint portraits of several of America's famous statesmen. Healey went to Lexington to do the portrait of Henry Clay, and he was a guest at Mr. Frazer's for a portion of his stay in Lexington. While staying in Mr. Frazer's home, Healey painted a portrait of himself, which he presented to his host. General Samuel Woodson Price has called this portrait "truly a masterpiece." Mr. Healey painted a portrait of Robert Frazer, but it was done after Mr. Frazer's death with a poor photograph as a guide, and it was not a good likeness.

Robert Frazer was not only a very successful businessman, but a man well known for his fine character and integrity. He died in 1851, a bachelor. He was succeeded in business by his nephew, Robert Frazer, Jr., the son of a brother in Ireland.

FRAZER, ROBERT, JR.

b.—Ireland
w. 1838-1851—Lexington

Robert Frazer, Jr., was a nephew of Robert and Alexander Frazer. He was born in Ireland but came to Lexington where he worked with his uncle, Robert Frazer, succeeding him in business at the southeast corner of Main and Upper Streets. He later moved to the country because of ill health.

Robert Frazer, Jr., was married in Louisville in April of 1831 to Miss Catharine E. Coleman. Two children are known to have been born of this marriage, a son and a daughter. Both died in infancy. The *Observer and Reporter*, on October 12, 1836, read: "Robert P. Frazer, son of Robert Frazer, Lexington. Died September 24, 1836, aged 4 years." Three days later the *Observer and Reporter* again carried sad news: "Eliza Coleman Frazer, daughter of Robert Frazer, of Lexington. She died September 27, 1836, aged 3 years."

The 1838-39 Lexington city directory lists Robert Frazer, Jr., as a watchmaker and jeweler. At least one set of teaspoons is known to exist marked "ROBERT FRAZER, JR."

FULTON, DAVID C.

w. 1838-1841—Louisville

David C. Fulton owned and operated a jewelry and fancy store in Louisville. In 1838 his shop was located at 14 East Main Street. In 1841 he had moved his business to Fourth Street, between Main and Market, and was living at the home of Mrs. Somer. Beverly Noel, a jeweler, was employed at Fulton's in 1838 and 1839.

FULTON, JAMES

w. 1838-1861—Louisville

James Fulton was a silversmith, watchmaker and jeweler. He is first listed in the Louisville city directory for 1838, and continues to appear continuously through 1861. According to the 1841 city directory he was employed by W. & A. Cooper, silversmiths. It would seem that he was in business for himself during the years with the exception of the short time he worked for the Coopers. He had several business addresses. In 1838 and 1839 he was located at 57 West Main Street. In 1843 he was on the west side of Fifth between Main and Market Streets. From 1845 until 1849 he was to be found at 99 Fourth, between Market and Jefferson Streets, and in 1851 he removed from 51 Fifth Street to the south side of Jefferson, between Fifth and Centre. Daniel Mead, silversmith, was employed at Fulton's in 1848.

GARNER, ELI C.

b. 1817

d. 1878—Lexington

w. 1838-1864—Lexington

Eli C. Garner was a silversmith, trained for his profession by Asa Blanchard. The exact time of his arrival in Lexington is not known. The 1838 Lexington city directory carries Eli Garner, silversmith, at Asa Blanchard's. At the time of Asa Blanchard's death in 1838 Eli C. Garner was twenty-one years of age. It was the express wish of Blanchard that Garner and George Easley, another Blanchard apprentice, go into partnership and he willed his tools to these two men. However, Blanchard's hopes did not materialize, for Easley left Lexington and Garner went into partnership with Mr. Winchester.

Eli C. Garner had two mulatto sons, George and Eli, both of whom had been trained in the business and were excellent engravers. Garner's son, Eli, left Lexington and no information concerning him has been found. However, George remained in Lexington where he worked as an engraver. For many years prior to his death, George was employed as an engraver by the Bogaert Jewelry Company in Lexington. According to Mr. Victor Bogaert, Jr., George Garner not only did beautiful engraving, but was a gold- and silversmith as well.

Eli C. Garner, jeweler and silversmith, was working at the corner of Main and Upper in 1864. The city directory for that year classified him as both a silversmith and a jeweler.

On January 28, 1878, E. C. Garner was interred in the Lexington Cemetery. He was sixty-one years old at the time of his death, and his residence is shown to have been "Lexington" on the cemetery's records.

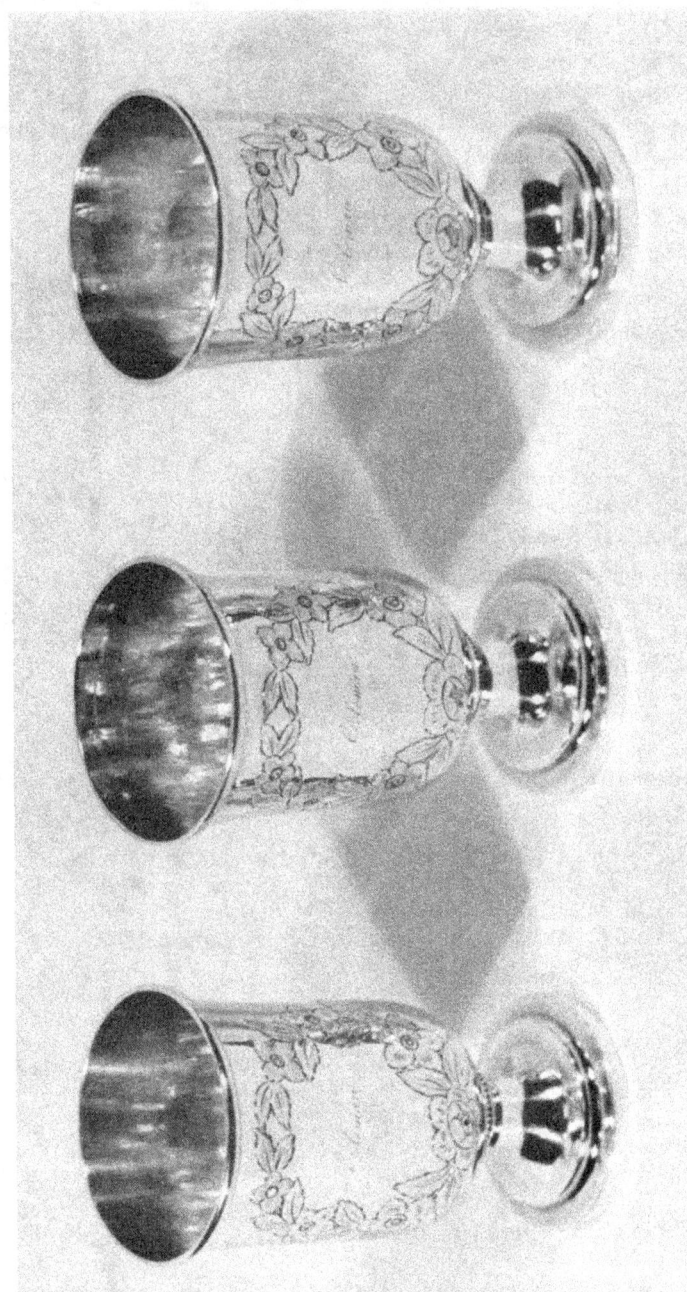

FOOTED SILVER CUPS

Matching footed silver cups bearing engraved family name "Coleman." Made by Garner and Winchester, Lexington. Owned by J. Winston Coleman, Jr.

GARNER AND WINCHESTER

w. 1838-1861—Lexington

Eli C. Garner, Sr., and a Mr. Winchester formed a partnership in 1838 and were in business at 6 Mill Street in Lexington until the Civil War. They did quite a fine business and during their years together made a great deal of beautiful, finely wrought silver.

GARNSEY, DAVID

w. 1810—Frankfort

David Garnsey was an early silversmith of Frankfort. He was advertising in the newspapers of Frankfort in 1810.

GILLASPIE, JOHN

w. 1845-1846—Louisville

d. 1875—Louisville

John Gillaspie was a silversmith who was working in Louisville in 1845 and 1846. He died in 1875 and was interred in Cave Hill Cemetery, Louisville, on February 8, 1875.

GILLESPIE, SAMUEL

w. 1848-1849—Louisville

Samuel Gillespie, a silversmith, appeared in the Louisville city directories in 1848 and 1849. His business location is not given, but he was living at 340 Main Street between Eighth and Ninth in 1848, and at 132 Market, between Fourteenth and Fifteenth in 1849.

GOETES, PETER

w. 1813-1844—Bardstown

Peter Goetes was an excellent silversmith. He was a Trappist Monk who had come to America from France with a company of laymen under the leadership of Father Urban. They had fled France during the Jacobin War in 1803. In 1813 Father Urban decided to return to France, but offered to release from their vows those in his group who wished to remain in America to practice their trades. Peter Goetes was one who stayed. He made his way, together with Felix F. Cachot and Ignatius Hottenroth, to Bardstown in Nelson County. Goetes (later called Gates) was a mere boy and learned the art of silversmithing and jeweler, as well as the trade of a watch- and clockmaker, from his friend and partner, Felix F. Cachot.

These three men, Goetes, Cachot and Hottenroth, arrived in Bardstown in 1813. In 1817 Goetes and Cachot made reciprocal wills. Cachot's will is recorded in the Nelson County Court House in Bardstown, but Goetes' will does not appear. Goetes outlived the other two men. Hottenroth was drowned a few years after arriving in Bardstown, and Cachot's will was probated on September 9, 1839.

Sometime after 1844 a stranger appeared in Bardstown. He convinced Peter Goetes fabulous fortunes were to be made in land in the State of Illinois. Goetes converted his entire wealth into cash and left Bardstown with the stranger. The story is that he very soon lost his entire fortune. No further record has been found of him. Peter Goetes was a mild mannered man with a quiet laugh who had "little to say but much to do."

GRAHAM, DR. CHRISTOPHER COLUMBUS

b. October 10, 1787—near Danville

w. 1812—Springfield

Christopher Columbus Graham was a silversmith. He opened a shop in Springfield and was plying his trade at the time of the War of 1812. He sold his few effects and used the money to personally recruit thirty men to whom he paid a bounty of $2.00 and $8.00 pay per month. He entered the war as a recruiting Sergeant in Springfield, Washington County, served a total of three years and participated in many engagements. He was wounded at the battle of Mackinaw.

After his release from the army in the War of 1812 he was involved for a short time in the War for Mexican Independence. He joined Mina at San Antonio, together with William Milam of Frankfort, Kentucky, another early silversmith.

Dr. Benjamin W. Dudley offered to finance Mr. Graham's education following his release from duty in the War of 1812, and C. C. Graham decided to take advantage of the generous offer. He graduated under Dr. Dudley's instruction, then went to Transylvania University where in a very short time he had completed his work. He then entered the study of medicine, becoming Dr. Christopher Columbus Graham. Dr. Graham had the distinction of being the first medical student graduated west of the Allegheny Mountains.

In 1822 Dr. Graham and Stephen Austin went to Mexico City to obtain a grant in Texas. Dr. Graham was there during the Civil War which removed Emperor Iturbide from the throne. General James Wilkinson had written a constitution for a new congressional government. By sewing this constitution between the soles of an old pair of brogan shoes, Dr. Graham succeeded in bringing it back through the opposing forces.

Dr. Graham owned large lead interests, was the owner of a boat navigating the Mississippi River, sold his well-known Graham Springs at Harrodsburg to the federal government for $100,000, went to Texas on an expedition concerning a railroad project and to examine iron and silver ore possibilities, and in the wilderness on Rockcastle River in Kentucky built "Sublimity," or Rockcastle Springs for which he had secured a charter. Here he spent ten years and $20,000 in erecting a hotel and cottages as well as a lumber and flouring mill. Dr. Graham opened roads to Somerset, Crab Orchard, Barbourville and London. He was also an author of note. At the age of eighty-two he published his finest work, "The Philosophy of the Mind." He was appointed director of many improvements and for twenty years gave generously of his time, knowledge and personal funds to these projects, among which were the turnpike from Lexington through Shakertown. He gave, and planted, the ground for the Presbyterian Female College at Harrodsburg; to the Christian Baptist Female College at Harrodsburg he gave a tract of twenty-four acres of land, then raised the money to rebuild the college when it burned down. He donated four acres of ground upon which was erected a fine residence for the President of Bacon College. At his own expense Dr. Graham graded the ground, sowed the grass seed and planted the trees around the Mercer County Court House. Harrodsburg's first graded and paved street was paid for by Dr. Graham.

This is but a partial account of his accomplishments and good works, yet he had arrived in Harrodsburg in 1819 with just $20, and this he had borrowed.

Dr. Graham was born on October 10, 1787, at his uncle's station four miles southeast of Danville, in what is now Boyle County. His uncle had come from Ireland, and served under General George Rogers Clark. Dr. Graham's mother was Irish. His father was a native of Virginia who moved to the Beach Fork in what is now Nelson County. He died when C. C. Graham was ten years old. Dr. Graham's grandfather was from the House of Montrose in Scotland.

Dr. Graham had two brothers, John and Robert, and all three became wealthy men. Robert, who died early in life, left a fortune of some $30,000. John, at the time of his death, was a judge and an elder in his church, and left an estate of $150,000. Dr. Graham retired before 1872, at which time his fortune amounted to $130,000.

GRANT, WILLIAM

w. 1808–Lexington

On May 9 1808, the Fayette County Court awarded to Asa Blanchard an apprentice named William Grant. It is possible that this man was a member of the firm of Smith and Grant which operated in Louisville from 1827 until August of 1831.

GRAY, THOMAS

w. 1818-1820—Lexington

Thomas Gray, silversmith, appears in the 1818 Lexington city directory, at which time he resided on Lowry Street, Western Suburbs. On the night of June 14, 1820, a raging fire destroyed his store on West Main Street. Mr. Gray and D. Curtis, both silversmiths, were among the eight businessmen who were completely ruined. The *Kentucky Reporter*, of June 21, 1820, carried the story of the disaster.

GRIFFIN, GEORGE

w. 1841-1852—Louisville

d. 1886—Louisville

George Griffin was a manufacturer of gold- and silverware. In 1841 he moved from the north side of Main Street between Sixth and Seventh, to Fourth Street between Market and Jefferson. By 1844 he was operating his shop on the east side of Fourth Street, between Main and Market. During 1848 and 1849 he was located at 680 Market, between Floyd and Preston, and in 1851 and 1852 we find him on Gray between Jackson and Hancock.

He employed other craftsmen in his shop. Edmund K. Burke, a jeweler; Samuel Caswell, a watchmaker; James Johnston, silversmith, and William Beggs, silversmith, were all working for him at one time.

On February 23, 1886, George Griffin was interred in Cave Hill Cemetery, Louisville.

GULICK, NATHAN

b. April 10, 1777—New Jersey

d. October 2, 1826—Maysville

w. 1818-1826—Maysville

Nathan Gulick was a silversmith and clockmaker who came to Maysville from Easton, Pennsylvania. He was born in New Jersey on April 10, 1777, the son of Samuel Gulick. He lived most of his adult life in Easton, Pennsylvania, where, in 1800, he married Elizabeth Erb, the daughter of Lawrence and Anna Maria (Driesback) Erb.

A resident of Harrisburg, Pennsylvania, has in her possession a beautifully made cherry grandfather clock which was made by Nathan Gulick. A descendant of Nathan Gulick owns a silver spoon made by him. Engraved on the handle of the spoon are the initials "N. & E. G.," for Nathan and Elizabeth Gulick. In Mason County Will Book

Y, page 526, there is an undated will which was probated August 8, 1898, which reads in part: ". . . to Martha J. Taylor one set of silver teaspoons made by Nathan Gulick and marked 'R. R. H.' [Rachel Runyon Hixson] on the handle."

The business ventures of Nathan Gulick were not confined to the making of fine silver and beautiful clocks. He also owned a sawmill as well as a stagecoach line running from Easton, Pennsylvania, to Philadelphia and Pittsburgh, in addition to taverns along the stagecoach route. Mr. Gulick and his brother-in-law, George Wolfe, the seventh Governor of Pennsylvania, owned a farm which they gave to Lafayette College at Easton, Pennsylvania.

Another descendant of Nathan Gulick is the proud owner of a lovely old clock which bears the name "S. Gulick." According to family tradition the clock was made by Samuel Gulick, father of Nathan Gulick.

An advertisement in the *Maysville Eagle* states that Nathan's father, Samuel Gulick, was in the jewelry business in Maysville with Pleasant H. Baird.

Nathan Gulick died on October 2, 1826, aged forty-nine years, five months and twenty-two days. He is buried in the oldest cemetery in Maysville, which is located back of the Maysville Public Library on Sutton Street.

HAIKES, HOLME

w. 1840–Paris

Holme (or Home) Haikes was a silversmith in Bourbon County. In 1840 he purchased the business of B. M. Riggs who had died in 1839. On February 21, 1840, H. Haikes advertised his business "at the stand of the late B. M. Riggs." On February 28, 1840, and thereafter, he spelled his last name "Hakes" in his advertising.

HAIR, JOSHUA J.

w. 1848–Louisville

Joshua J. Hair employed Milton McConothy, a silversmith, according to the 1848 Louisville city directory.

HALEY, G. W. or P.

c. 1850–Paris

The firm of Haley and Haley, composed of P. Haley and G. W. Haley, was doing business in Paris, Kentucky, in 1855. Silver has been seen marked "HALEY," which would indicate that at least one of these men was operating alone prior to the time of the partnership.

HALL, JOHN
w. 1848—Louisville

John Hall, a silversmith, was working at 37 Eighth Street, between Main and Market, in 1848.

HALLACK, ALONZO CORWIN
w. 1840-1853—Paris

A. C. Hallack was a silversmith working in Paris in 1840. He no doubt was making silver in that city prior to 1840.

Aria Harrison Newman (Mrs. Charles William) of Indianapolis owns five teaspoons marked "A. C. HALLACK" "PARIS, KY." The spoons were purchased in 1842 by Aria Kennedy Talbott for a gift to her granddaughter, Aria Talbott, born in 1842. The spoons bear the engraved initials "A.T." for Aria Talbott, who died in 1859 at the age of seventeen. The spoons were then given to her niece, Aria Thomas (Hinamon), who is now eighty years of age, and she in turn gave them to her niece, Aria Harrison Newman, about 1950. This information was gleaned from the family Bible and other family records.

The maker's mark on his spoons would indicate that Mr. Hallack worked alone prior to his partnership with L. Matthews, which partnership was in existence in 1852.

Mrs. Wade Hampton Whitley of Paris advises that the Hallack family came to Kentucky from Virginia and that the descendants living in Bourbon County use the spelling "Halleck." Miss Elizabeth Steele of Lexington, a descendant of Thomas Hallack and his first wife, Susannah Jacoby, advises they use the spelling "Hallack." She further states: "I have a hazy recollection of an old will mentioning land in Lincoln County. The first Hallack in this county settled on Long Island in the old Hallack home which I believe still exists. He (Alonzo) married the widow Howell...." Miss Steele also advises that Alonzo Corwin Hallack was a son of Benjamin Hallack and his second wife, Polly Cown. In 1840 Polly Hallack advertised that B. Hallack's heirs offered three hundred and fifty acres of land for sale, which establishes the date of 1840 as the probable time of death for this craftsman's father. Alonzo's first wife was Ann Carpenter of Lincoln County. They had a daughter, Annie, who married a Mr. Wisdom of Huntsville, Missouri.

In 1841 Alonzo Hallack had the following account with the Marsh brothers, silversmiths of Paris, Kentucky:

"1841 Mr. Alonzo Hallack   Dr.
Feb. 12   To one gold fob chane   26.00
Ap. 19   "   " pencil case   2.00
Aug. 21   "   clean & Rep watch   1.50
  " "   "   mend B pin   .12½
  " 30   "   Watch glass   .50   30.12½

Dec. 27   Cred by Note   30.12½   30.12½"

A. C. Hallack was still advertising in the *Western Citizen* in 1853.

HANSBROUGH, HAMLET

c. 1800-1839—Lexington

Hamlet Hansbrough was a watchmaker and jeweler. Mr. Charles R. Staples, of Lexington, advises that H. Hansbrough arrived in Lexington in 1800. In the 1838-39 Lexington city directory Hamlet Hansbrough is listed as a watchmaker and jeweler, with his place of business at 7 Main Street. He lived on Constitution Street at the corner of Walnut.

HARDMAN, JACOB N.

w. 1845-1849—Louisville

Jacob N. Hardman was a silversmith, a jeweler and a watch- and clockmaker in Louisville. The 1845-46 Louisville city directory shows him on Fifteenth Street at the corner of Green. He was working at Hudson's as a silversmith in 1848, but by 1849 he was in business alone on Fourth Street between Main and Water.

HARDMAN, WILLIAM

w. 1838-1840—Lexington

William Hardman was a very versatile man. He was a jeweler, a manufacturer of silverware, and a surgeon dentist. Following the death of Asa Blanchard, Hardman took over Blanchard's former business at the corner of Mill and Short Streets. An advertisement in the *Observer & Reporter,* for January 1, 1840, shows that he "... is now manufacturing every description of JEWELRY and SILVER WARE of the best style." The 1838-39 Lexington city directory carried his advertisement in which he advertised himself as a "surgeon dentist," with his dental office at Jordan's Row, 12 N. Upper Street, between Main and Short Streets.

Spoons have been seen bearing the mark "W. HARDMAN" "LEX. KY." Mrs. John Pack of Georgetown bought a beautiful silver cup in the southern part of Louisiana from a family which moved there from Lexington, Kentucky. This cup, too, bears W. Hardman's mark.

HARRIS, JOHN C.

w. 1831-1836—Louisville

John C. Harris is listed as a jeweler in the Louisville city directory. He was a brother of Mr. Alfred Harris who for many years was Assessor for the City of Louisville.

On November 2, 1831, the *Louisville Daily Focus* advised: "The partnership of John C. Harris and James I. Lemon was dissolved November 2, 1831 . . ." Later in 1831 Mr. Harris formed a partnership with William Kendrick, but this partnership was dissolved in less than one year. In 1836 Mr. Harris was working as a jeweler at R. E. Smith's store in Louisville.

HARRIS AND KENDRICK

w. 1831-1832—Louisville

Mr. Harris and William Kendrick formed a partnership in 1831, but it was short lived. Less than one year later the partnership was dissolved.

HASSAN, MOSES

w. 1848-1852—Louisville

Moses Hassan was a jeweler and a watchmaker, and was listed in the Louisville city directories from 1848 to 1852. His last name was spelled "Hassan" in two of the directories and "Hessen" in another. He operated his business on Market Street between Sixth and Seventh Streets.

HEADINGTON, WILLIAM

w. 1806-1807—Frankfort

William Headington, silversmith and jeweler, advertised in the *Western World* of Frankfort on July 19 and August 9, 1806:

> "HEADINGTON, WILLIAM—Watch maker, silver smith and jeweler, intends moving to Frankfort in about 3 weeks, Where he will commence the above business in all its various branches, in the house in the lower part of the Town formerly occupied by Willis A. Lee and nearly opposite to Dr. Scott's."

Again, on March 26, 1807, he advertised in the *Western World:*

> "HEADINGTON, WILLIAM to move his Watch shop from here. Shop kept now at James Roberts."

Where his home had been, or in what locality he operated his business before coming to Frankfort is not known. His stay in Frankfort was a brief one, and he moved on to parts unknown.

HENSLEY, SAMUEL

w. 1829-1833—Mt. Sterling

Samuel Hensley was an early silversmith who worked in Mt. Sterling. His marriage, on December 31, 1794, to Allefer Cooper, the daughter of Leven Cooper, is recorded in the First Shelby County Marriage Bond Record of 1794, and he was entered on the Shelby County Tax List under date of March 24, 1796, which reads "50 Acres (2 rate), Watercorse whar the land lies . . ."

In 1829 David M. Spurgin, a lad of fifteen, was apprenticed to Samuel Hensley. Spurgin later worked as a journeyman, gaining in skill and experience. In 1833 D. M. Spurgin purchased Samuel Hensley's stock in Mt. Sterling, moved it to Carlisle, and went into business for himself.

HICKMAN, JOHN

w. 1836—Louisville

John Hickman, a silversmith, was working in Louisville in 1836. His shop was on the west side of Wall, between Main and Water Streets. More exact dates for him are not known, but it appears he also worked in Spencer, Nelson and other counties. The authors have seen teaspoons, owned by Mrs. Rebecca J. Talbott of Bardstown, which were made by Hickman. A Captain Hickman was interred in Lexington Cemetery, January 31, 1863, but the body was removed February 1, 1864.

HINTON, WILLIAM M.

b. 1830

w. 1844-1847—Paris

w. 1847-1854—Shelbyville

w. 1854-   —Paris

William Hinton, born in 1830, learned the trade of silversmith from Benedict Beal Marsh of Paris, Kentucky, according to Miss Jane Marsh, a descendant of Marsh. He worked with B. B. Marsh in Paris for three years, then went to Shelbyville in 1847 where he worked for seven years, returning in 1854 to Paris where he was in business with E. Clark, Jr. William M. Hinton was probably the last silversmith working in Paris.

The *Kentuckian-Citizen* of Paris contained a news item that William Hinton became associated with Mr. Marsh in 1844, learned the trade and in 1854, when Mr. Marsh retired to the farm, Mr. Hinton took over the business and became one of the outstanding silversmiths and jewelers of Bourbon and adjoining counties. Again, in the *Kentuckian-Citizen:* "The late William Hinton, who for many years conducted a jewelry and repair shop in Paris was taught his trade by the Marshes." The two news items referred to have been seen by the authors, but they were not dated.

HITER, JOHN G.

w. 1813—Lexington

John Hiter was a silversmith who spent several years working with skilled craftsmen in many places before entering into partnership with Samuel Ayres in Lexington on June 3, 1813. The partnership was dissolved before 1819, at which time Mr. Ayres was advertising alone.

HORTON, H. V.

w. 1848—Louisville

H. V. Horton was a jeweler in Louisville, and his place of business was situated at the corner of Fifth and Walnut. The 1848 Louisville city directory lists him as "jeweller, etc."

HUDSON, HENRY

w. 1841-1856—Louisville

d. 1888—Louisville

Henry Hudson was a goldsmith, silversmith and jeweler who conducted a large and prosperous business in Louisville for many years. He arrived in Louisville in 1841, and was listed in the Louisville city directories continuously until 1856. He was in partnership with Jacob Dolfinger during 1855 and 1856. From 1841 to 1844 his shop was on the west side of Wall near Main Street. By 1845 he was carrying on his business at 64 Fourth, and residing at 307 Green Street.

During his business career he employed many gold- and silversmiths. Some of them were Jacob Dolfinger who worked for him seven years, Friederich Dolfinger, William Brown, William O. Atkinson, Jacob N. Hardman, Thomas Orr and John Park. Henry Hudson was both a retail and a wholesale manufacturer of silver articles.

He was interred in Cave Hill Cemetery, Louisville, on May 16, 1888.

HUMPHREYS, DAVID

w. 1789-1793—Lexington

David Humphreys, a man of many talents, advertised in *The Kentucky Gazette* on June 6, and June 13, 1789:

> **"DAVID HUMPHREYS**
> **Clock and Watch Maker**
>
> Most respectfully informs the public, that he lives near the new court house, at the sign of the Buffalo, where he carries on the clock and watch making business, in all its various branches. Merchants, and others, may be furnished with labels, or any kind of device, neatly engraved copper, and printed on the most reasonable terms. Also Devices in hair, for rings, lockets, etc., executed in a neat and elegant manner."

Mr. Charles R. Staples of Lexington advises he has seen one piece of his work—a beautiful bowl twelve inches in diameter, with "curled edges."

Four years later, David Humphreys was singularly honored when, on July 10, 1793, he was awarded the sum of twelve pounds sterling in payment for his having made the first seal and press for the Commonwealth of Kentucky.

The Harrison County Order Book A records that Polly Coleman and Covington Coleman, orphans of Francis Coleman, deceased, chose David Humphreys as their guardian.

HUMPHREYS, JOSHUA

1785—Lexington

d. November 23, 1823—Lexington

Joshua Humphreys was probably the first silversmith to arrive in Kentucky. He came to Kentucky from Virginia in 1785. Several thousand acres in land grants were entered in his name in 1783 before he moved to his new home. He died in Lexington on November 23, 1823.

HYMAN, HENRY W.

w. 1799—Lexington

Henry W. Hyman was a gold- and silversmith who came to America from England. On May 23, 1799, *The Kentucky Gazette* of Lexington carried the following advertisement:

"HENRY HYMAN
Gold and Silversmith, Clock and Watch Maker
(from London)

Begs leave to inform his friends and the public, that he has served a regular apprenticeship to the above business, in Great Britain, that he has opened shop in Lexington in the house of Mr. William Ross, on Short Street, where he intends working in the above lines, in all their branches. Those who may please to employ him may depend on the utmost punctuality and reasonable terms.

Lexington, January 21st, 1799"

ILLIG, G. P. H.

w. 1836—Louisville

The silversmith, G. P. H. Illig, was listed in the 1836 Louisville city directory, working on the west side of Fifth Street, between Main and Market. He appeared in this directory only.

IRION, MATT

Louisville

The only reference to this man found so far is contained in William Carnes Kendrick's "Memoir To My Father William Kendrick" in his *Reminiscences Of Old Louisville*. In this publication Mr. Kendrick mentions Matt Irion, the jeweler, whose father-in-law was B. T. Kluth, a German, who manufactured and repaired jewelry on Fourth Street near Market, and who did work for William Kendrick.

IRWIN, MASON T.

w. 1838-1839—Louisville

Mason T. Irwin, a jeweler, was in business in Louisville in 1838. The directory shows he was located on Green Street at the corner of Seventh.

IZABELL, JOHN

w. 1818—Lexington

John Izabell, a jeweler, is found in Lexington's second city directory, published in 1818. His place of business was on Main Street.

JAMESON, JOHN D.

c. 1823

John D. Jameson was a silversmith as well as a farmer and tobacco merchant, of Scottish origin. His mother, Eliza Coleman, was a native of Kentucky whose parents had come from Virginia. John D. Jameson was born in Orange County, Virginia. His son, Robert Coleman Jameson, was born March 8, 1823. He clerked in Trenton, Kentucky, for three years, then worked with an uncle at Cadiz in Trigg County, later returning to Trenton. He was the founder of the town of Pembroke in Christian County, adjoining the Tennessee line ten miles southeast of Hopkinsville. Just when or where he followed the trade of silversmithing has not been determined.

JANUARY, ANDREW McCONNELL

b. August 3, 1794—Jessamine County
d. June 11, 1877—Maysville
w. 1812-1818—Lexington

Andrew McConnell January received his training in the silversmith's business in Lexington, where, beginning in 1812, he served three and one-half years as an apprentice. Early in 1816 he opened his own business in Lexington, residing at what is now known as 900 North Broadway. The house still stands and is in use today. He abandoned his trade in Lexington in 1818, moving to Maysville where he engaged in the produce, grocery and commission business. In 1848 he purchased an interest in the cotton mills in Maysville, continuing in that business, with his partner B. W. Wood, until his death in 1877. The January-Wood Company is still in business today manufacturing carpet warp.

Andrew M. January was born August 3, 1794, in Jessamine County, Kentucky. His father, Ephraim January, was born in Pennsylvania and was of French Huguenot extraction. Ephraim January moved to Kentucky in 1780. During the first three years in Kentucky he lived at the fort at Lexington, moving in 1783 to Jessamine County. Andrew January's mother, Sarah McConnell, was the daughter of Andrew McConnell, an early pioneer who settled in Kentucky in 1775 and who was slain in 1782 by the Indians during the battle of Blue Licks.

Andrew McConnell January received little education, and left the farm to learn the art of silversmithing in Lexington. He proved to be a successful businessman, and in 1829 was elected a director of the Maysville and Lexington Turnpike. He served as a director of the Lexington Branch of the United States Bank and was the first President of the Maysville Branch of the Bank of Kentucky, and also President of its successor, the Bank of Kentucky in Maysville. He was Vice-President of the Maysville and Lexington Railroad Company, Northern Division. Later he subscribed $20,000 to the successor of this company, but lost this investment. A. M. January played a large part in the progress of Maysville. He owned a fine residence there, a block of business buildings, made improvements to the cotton mills, and played a leading role in the establishing and financing of the Presbyterian Church and the Court House. He made generous contributions to many worthwhile projects, including the Presbyterian Church and Centre College in Danville. He served his church as deacon and later as an elder for more than half a century.

On December 31, 1816, he married Sarah Huston of Lexington. They had thirteen children, but only two of them survived the parents. Andrew McConnell January died June 11, 1877, in Maysville. Will Book X, page 91, in the Mason County Court Record, records his will which was dated October 1, 1874, and proven June 14, 1877.

JANUARY AND NUTMAN

w. 1818—Lexington

The firm of January and Nutman, silver platers, were in business on Main Street in Lexington in 1818.

JEFFRIES, JAMES

w. 1820-1860—Glasgow

James Jeffries was a silversmith in Glasgow, Barren County. He may have worked in Winchester at some time during his career, but this has not been definitely established. The Barren County Marriage Records in Glasgow record his marriage to Rebecca Eubank in 1822.

JEFFRIES, SMITH

c. 1825-1835—Winchester

Smith Jeffries was a silversmith. From 1829 to 1833 he employed David M. Spurgin, silversmith, who worked with him as a journeyman. After that time Smith Jeffries carried on his trade in Winchester.

JOHNSON, SAMUEL (or Simeon) W.

w. 1836-1844—Louisville

S. W. Johnson, a jeweler, was carried in the Louisville city directories from 1836 to 1844. In 1836 he was located on the west side of Fourth Street, between Main and Market where he continued until 1843 when he moved to the west side of Seventh Street, between Walnut and Chestnut.

JOHNSTON, JAMES

w. 1812-1843—Louisville

James Johnston was a silversmith who enjoyed the privilege of plying his trade for many years. In 1812 L. L. Tod listed "James Johnston, Silversmith" on the roll of the Lexington Light Infantry which was under the command of Captain N. G. Hart in the War of 1812.

The Louisville city directories for the years 1841 to 1844 list James Johnston as a silversmith, during which period he was employed at George Griffin's shop.

KEEVE, G. H.

w. 1848-1849—Louisville

Nothing is known of this man except that he did appear in the Louisville city directory for 1848-49. He does not appear in the alphabetical listing of the directory, but is included under the heading of "Jewelers."

KENDRICK, WILLIAM

b. February 11, 1810—Paterson, New Jersey
d. March 16, 1880—Louisville
w. 1824-1880—Louisville

William Kendrick was a jeweler in Louisville for a great many years. From a lonely and struggling beginning he became, by his own initiative and integrity, an acknowledged success in his chosen business career.

William Kendrick's father, Walter Kendrick, was born at Sandon, near Stone, in Staffordshire, England, September 16, 1765. In 1795 Walter Kendrick married Nancy Fielding near Manchester, England, and very soon after their marriage he left his bride in England and came to America to establish himself in business. He arrived in New York in 1796 and before very long wrote his waiting wife: ". . . have now got quite fixed in a very good stand for business . . . . I have the neatest hat shop in the city and the newest fashions from London." William Penton Kendrick of Louisville now owns the original letter, which was written in June of 1797. The paper was folded to permit an overlap to be sealed with sealing wax, as was the custom of the day.

William Kendrick, one of four children, was born February 11, 1810, in Paterson, New Jersey. On September 23, 1813, when he was three years of age, his mother died. Five years later his father moved the family to Louisville, where on April 2, 1819, he married Mrs. Elizabeth McMullen. His father and stepmother died within ten days of each other. Mrs. Kendrick died in Louisville on September 7, 1822, and Walter Kendrick died in Texas, a victim of malaria, on September 17, 1822. William Kendrick was thus left an orphan at the age of thirteen with no one to provide for his support.

For a time he lived with a Mr. Jones, but desiring to provide for himself, he went to Bardstown where he worked at the Village Inn. On July 5, 1824, William Kendrick became a jeweler's apprentice to E. C. Beard in Louisville. He served his seven-year apprenticeship well and at the age of twenty-one he began his first business venture. He formed a partnership with a Mr. Harris in 1831, but this partnership was dissolved a year later.

On November 1, 1831, he formed a partnership with James Innes Lemon, a man six years his senior. The *Louisville Daily Focus* of November 2, 1831, carried the announcement of the formation of this new partnership, advising business would be continued at the "old stand opposite Bull and Casedy's" where the firm of Harris and Lemon had conducted their business. According to the city directory, this location was at Main and Fourth Streets. The partnership of Lemon and Kendrick continued for ten years. The firm moved to the south side of Main Street, west of Third, in 1837. The two men were friends of long standing as well as partners in business. They prospered and the future looked very promising. Then came the financial disaster of 1839 which brought their business to an abrupt halt, forcing the firm into bankruptcy in 1841. The partnership was never re-established, but at the earliest possible time, each man went into business for himself, and both repaid their creditors in full, including interest. The New York creditors presented William Kendrick with a beautiful silver pitcher which bore the following inscription:

> "Presented to William Kendrick, of Louisville, Kentucky, by Fellows, Wadsworth & Co., Fellows, Cargill & Co., Francis Tomes & Sons, and Downing & Baldwin, of New York; as a testimonial of their esteem for his integrity and moral worth. An honest man's the noblest work of God."

The first ledger of Lemon and Kendrick carries among the account entries the names of Richard E. Smith, E. C. Beard and Co., Milton McConothy and others, which is indicative of this firm's fine reputation.

Mr. Kendrick reopened his business in his original location, where he remained until 1856, when he moved to the east side of Third, between Market and Main Streets, continuing there until the Civil War. In 1870 he built and occupied a brown stone-front store on the south side of Main Street, and five years later he had rented the corner store in a block of new stone-front shops. Here he remained until his death in 1880.

William Kendrick married Maria Schwing (daughter of John G. Schwing, a silversmith) on January 19, 1832. He was twenty-one years of age, and his bride just past her seventeenth birthday. Maria's parents built their home on the northwest corner of Seventh and Walnut in 1832. William Kendrick's wife owned a lot on the north side of Walnut, a few doors west of Seventh Street, and here he built their lovely brick home. They lived here but a few years, for when financial destruction came, their home as well as their business was given up in order to reimburse their creditors as far as possible. They had nine children—six daughters and three sons.

There are three old catalogues in existence which show that William Kendrick and James I. Lemon were in partnership from 1832 to 1841; from 1841 until 1878 William Kendrick was the sole owner of his establishment, but in 1878 William C. Kendrick was admitted as a partner, and the firm name became "Wm. Kendrick and Son." After the death of William Kendrick in 1880 the firm was composed of W. C. Kendrick and George P. Kendrick, the firm then becoming "Wm. Kendrick's Sons." Today, one hundred and twenty-two years later, the firm established by William Kendrick in 1831 is still in existence.

William Kendrick employed many craftsmen through the years, including Mr. Barnes, a heavy-set Englishman who made an enormous amount of silver for Mr. Kendrick; William Drysdale, Alfred A. Dumont, and others.

The records of the Calvary Church in Louisville show that, at the time the church was planning their new building on Fourth Street, they discovered a few more feet of ground would be necessary to complete their structure as planned. William Kendrick, who owned the adjoining property, let them have the necessary eight feet of land, thus making it possible for their project to be completed. Mr. Kendrick was deeply interested in the Kentucky School for the Blind and served for many years as a member of its board. A portrait of him now hangs at the school.

William Kendrick's jewelry store was long known as the "House of Spoons" because of the six large wooden spoons which hung in his display window. They were first placed in the window about 1835 or 1840, and are still in the possession of the Kendrick family.

W. C. Kendrick, son of the firm's founder, has written that frequently he found merchants from other parts of the state waiting for the store to be opened. They came with orders for spoons, watches and jewelry which they purchased for their home-town customers.

The death of William Kendrick came on March 16, 1880. Both the *Courier-Journal* and the *Evening Post and News* of March 17, 1880, carried the announcement:

> "Died at his residence on Broadway, near Sixth street, in the city of Louisville, at twenty minutes past 10 o'clock, on the night of the 16th of March, 1880, of Angina Pectoris, William Kendrick aged 70 years, 1 month and 5 days."

Funeral services were held at the Methodist Church on Chestnut Street, and interment was in Cave Hill Cemetery in Louisville.

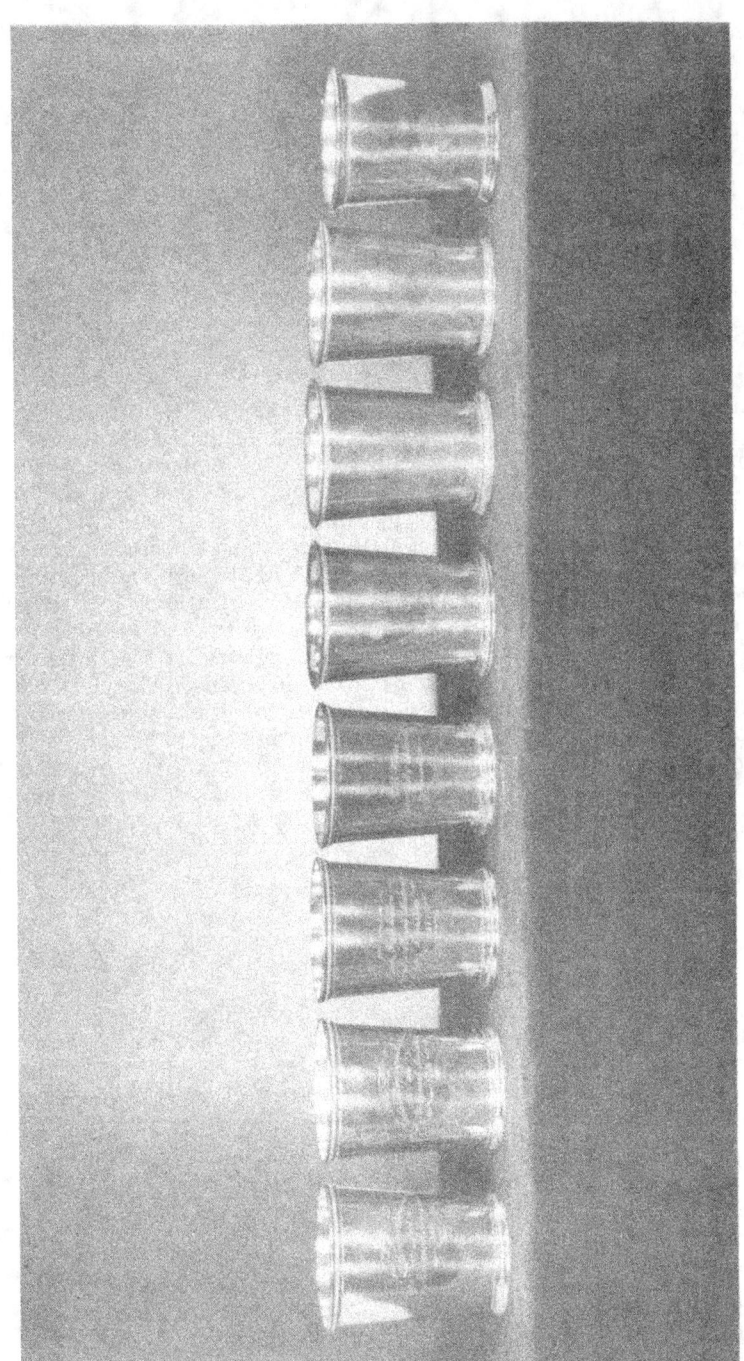

SILVER CUPS

Left to right: 4 cups, John Kitts, Louisville; 2 cups, Hudson and Dolfinger, Louisville; 1 cup, Henry Hudson, Louisville; 1 cup, John B. Akin, Danville. Owned by Katherine Wakefield Gilliatt (Mrs. C. E.).

KINSEY, EDWARD

w. 1834-1836—Newport

Edward Kinsey was born in North Wales, Ireland. He and his brother, David, have been considered silversmiths of Cincinnati, Ohio. Mrs. Wade Hampton Whitley of Paris, Kentucky, has advised, however, that Edward Kinsey was working in Newport, Kentucky, in 1834 and boarding at the Newport Hotel. In 1836 he moved across the river and continued his profession in Cincinnati.

KITTS, JOHN

w. 1836-1874—Louisville

John Kitts was a goldsmith, silversmith, watchmaker and jeweler. From 1836 to 1841 he was employed by Lemon and Kendrick as a watchmaker. In 1843 and 1844 John Kitts was in partnership with a Mr. Scott, but in 1845 he was working alone at 60 Fourth Street. The 1851-52 Louisville city directory lists the firm of Kitts and Stoy, but this partnership was of short duration. During the years 1851 through 1874 John Kitts was in partnership with both Joseph Werne, Sr., and Joseph Werne, Jr. John Kitts had a long and active business career in Louisville and there is a great deal of silver to be found today bearing his name, or that of one of the firms in which he was a partner. The firms listed in Louisville's early city directories make it apparent that John Kitts was a member of more than one partnership at the same time during some of the years covering his business career. The firm of Kitts and Werne was in operation from 1865 until 1874. John Kitts and Company were in business from 1851 until 1871.

KLINK, JOHN J.

w. 1841-1859—Louisville

d. October, 1900—Louisville

John J. Klink was another craftsman of many talents. He was employed by Henry Fletcher as a silversmith, jeweler and watchmaker, and the Louisville city directory continues to list him until 1859. John J. Klink died in 1900 and was interred in Cave Hill Cemetery on November 1, 1900.

KLUTH, B. T.

Louisville

B. T. Kluth was a German who manufactured and repaired jewelry in his shop on the second floor of a small house near Market Street. He did a great amount of work for William Kendrick. His daughter married Matt Irion, a jeweler of Louisville.

KNOX, HENRY

w. 1848—Louisville

Henry Knox was a silver plater who appeared only once in the city directory. Nothing further has been learned concerning him. During his stay in Louisville he boarded with a family named Fayseaux.

LEA, FRANCIS

1789—Fayette County

d. September 9, 1805, Frankfort

The first record of Francis Lea, the silversmith, appears in the *First Census of Kentucky*, in which he was recorded in Fayette County, July 2, 1789. He later went to Frankfort where he died on Monday morning, September 9, 1805. He was still a young man at the time of his death.

LEMON, JAMES INNES

  b. 1804—Georgetown

  d. 1869—Louisville

  a. 1825—Lexington

  w. 1828-1869—Louisville

James I. Lemon was a silversmith who served his apprenticeship under Asa Blanchard in Lexington. In 1825, during the time J. I. Lemon was in Lexington, General Lafayette, then an old man, visited the city and Mr. Lemon was a member of the committee appointed to receive him.

He went to Louisville in 1828 where he established his business on Main Street. One year after his arrival in Louisville Mr. Lemon married Fayette Taylor, a relative of President Zachary Taylor. In 1830 he formed a partnership with John C. Harris. This partnership was dissolved on November 2, 1831, and at the same time a new partnership with William Kendrick was formed. From 1831 until 1841 Lemon and Kendrick continued in business, and during the ten years together, as friends and partners, they prospered. Due, however, to the financial panic of the country during 1838 to 1842 these two men were forced into bankruptcy, necessitating the cessation of business operations in 1841. The partnership was never re-established, but each man later began business alone, and in a matter of a few years had succeeded in paying their creditors in full, with interest, even though they had no legal obligation to do so.

The 1844 Louisville city directory carried James I. Lemon under WATCH, CLOCK, JEWELRY AND SILVERSMITHS. The following year Mr. Lemon advertised:

"JAMES I. LEMON
No. 63 Fourth, between Main and Market
Dealer In

Watches, Chains, Seals, Keys, Brestpins, Finger and Ear Rings, Gold and Silver Pencils, Silver, Plates, and Britannia Ware, Solar Lard Lamps of every description, Pocket Knives and Scissors, together with a variety of other Goods. Perifocal Glasses, in Gold and Silver Frames.

Old Gold and Silver taken in exchange for Goods. Watches and Clocks carefully Repaired."

From 1859 to 1861 James I. Lemon was in partnership with Edmund J. Daumont under the firm name of James I. Lemon and Co. In 1862 the firm moved to Fourth and Green Streets at which time James K. Lemon was taken into the business, the firm name then becoming James I. Lemon and Son. The company continued under this name until the death of James I. Lemon in 1869. The business begun by James Innes Lemon in 1828 is still in existence today, and is one of the few firms which have been in business for more than a century and a quarter.

James Innes Lemon was born in Georgetown, Scott County, Kentucky, in 1804. He died in 1869. His grandfather, Captain James Lemon, was a Scotch-Irish patriot who died in the Battle of Brandywine during the Revolutionary War.

LEMON AND KENDRICK
w. 1831-1841—Louisville

On November 2, 1831, *The Louisville Daily Focus* carried the following announcement:

> "The partnership of John C. Harris and James I. Lemon was dissolved November 2, 1831" and "partnership formed at the same time with William Kendrick and business continued at the old stand opposite Bull and Casedy's under the firm name of Lemon and Kendrick."

"The old stand" was at Main and Fourth Streets, according to the city directory. It was here they carried on an excellent and a growing business for ten years, offering to the buying public an outstanding assortment of jewelry, clocks, watches, silver and other allied items. Financial tragedy, however, was to be responsible for terminating the partnership of these two friends. During the years from 1838 to 1842 the country as a whole experienced such financial disaster that business failures were the rule of the day. Lemon and Kendrick were forced into bankruptcy in 1841. A short time later each man opened his own business establishment. Each began on the proverbial "shoe

1832 LEMON AND KENDRICK LEDGER

1832 Ledger showing accounts with Lemon and Kendrick of Louisville during the firm's first year. Owned by William Kendrick Jewelers, Inc.

string," but in the space of a few years they were able to make payment in full, with interest, to their former creditors. Legally they had no further obligation following their enforced entry into bankruptcy, but such was the integrity and character of these two men that they did not rest until they had made settlement in full.

John Kitts was employed by this firm from 1838 to 1841, and Benjamin H. McGehee, a watchmaker, worked for the firm during 1838 and 1839.

LOOMIS, WORHAM P.
w. 1819-1854—Frankfort

Early in his career Worham P. Loomis, silversmith, was in partnership with a Mr. Ralph in Frankfort. In the latter years of his business activity in Frankfort Mr. Loomis was in business with a Mr. Conery. However, for many years W. P. Loomis was in the silversmith and jewelry business alone.

During 1838 and 1839 W. P. Loomis advertised in the *Frankfort Commonwealth* that he did watch and clock repairing at Mr. Conery's Jewelry Store. By 1846 he had his own shop and on November 17, 1846, advertised: "W. P. Loomis, jewelry. Few doors east of Mansion House."

A short time later ill health necessitated his temporary retirement from business. On August 31, 1852, the *Commonwealth* carried the announcement: "W. P. Loomis, owing to ill health is desirous of retiring from watch making business." Less than two years later Mr. Loomis advertised the reopening of his business, but difficulties continued to arise. In May of 1854 *The Tri-Weekly Commonwealth* carried an article describing the losses sustained by several businessmen in Frankfort as the result of a fire, in which W. P. Loomis lost his property. Most of the contents were saved, and the $1,200 insurance which he carried fully covered his loss.

Two days after the fire Mr. Loomis had located in "the corner room opposite the Capital Hotel formerly occupied by a barber shop." He made still another move within a few days, for on May 16, 1854, he advertised: "W. P. Loomis, Silversmith, has reopened near the corner of Main and Ann, diagonally opposite the Capital Hotel and next door above Evans and Company Book Store."

Many Kentucky residents, as well as out-of-state descendants of Kentucky's early pioneers, own silver bearing the mark of W. P. Loomis, Frankfort. Katherine Wakefield Gilliatt (Mrs. C. E.) of Seymour, Indiana, owns a huge ladle, a smaller ladle, tablespoons and teaspoons made by W. P. Loomis of Frankfort, which were originally owned by her great-grandparents, Nancy Grubbs Crutcher and Thomas Graves Crutcher of Franklin County, Kentucky, who were married on April 18, 1849. Their daughter, Laura Boone Crutcher, was Mrs. Gilliatt's grandmother. Half of the silver is engraved "N.G.C." (Nancy Grubbs Crutcher) and the other half is engraved "T.G.C." (Thomas Graves Crutcher). Nancy and Thomas Crutcher were descendants of hardy pioneers who came to Kentucky from Virginia. Many of their ancestors fought in the Revolutionary War, among them being Capt. James Harris, Capt. Higgason Grubbs, George Boone (a brother of Daniel Boone) and Abner Wilson of Nancy Grubbs (Wilson) Crutcher's family, with Thomas Graves, William Beasley, Capt. John Hancock and Henry Crutcher, Jr., of Thomas Graves Crutcher's family. The silver cups illustrated on page 53 also belonged to Thomas Graves Crutcher, having been awarded to him in 1855 as prizes for fine cattle.

W. P. Loomis has been described as "a very eccentric but splendid and efficient workman." When he became too old personally to direct his business, Mr. Conery, Captain W. B. Thompson and George W. Gayle carried on for him until his death, at which time the business was closed.

LOOMIS AND RALPH

w. 1819–Frankfort

This partnership of silversmiths advertised in Frankfort newspapers in 1819. How long the firm continued has not been determined, but W. P. Loomis was advertising alone in 1838, which would indicate that the partnership had been dissolved by that time.

LOVE, JAMES

w. 1832-1836–Louisville

James Love appeared as a silversmith in Louisville's first city directory, published in 1832. At that time he was located on Fifth Street near Market. He also appeared in the 1836 directory, being listed as a silversmith on the south side of Market, between Fifth and Sixth Streets.

MAHIN, THOMAS S.

1819-1880–Franklin

Little is known of this early craftsman other than the fact that he worked in Simpson County. The Simpson County Court Clerk has advised that the Court House burned in 1882, destroying all records prior to that time.

MARSH, BENEDICT BEAL
b. 1804—Bourbon County
d. 1875—Bourbon County
w. Flemingsburg, Richmond and Paris

Benedict Beal Marsh was a silversmith and clockmaker of Bourbon County. He was born in 1804 on his father's farm just one mile outside Paris, Kentucky. Farming did not interest him, and he soon was launched upon a career of his own. He went to Philadelphia where he learned the silversmith's art. Upon his return to Kentucky he worked for a while in Flemingsburg, then went to Richmond, and finally located permanently in Paris. At the age of nineteen he lost one leg by amputation. He and his brother, Thomas King Marsh, worked together for many years, and it was B. B. Marsh who taught William M. Hinton the trade of silversmith.

Benedict Beal Marsh's father, Beal Marsh, and his mother, Eleanor Corbin Marsh, were born in Maryland. Eleanor Corbin Marsh died on May 19, 1810 and Beal Marsh died on November 5, 1835. They had six children—Dryden (b. 1798), Abram C., Nicholas C., Thomas K., Rachel (married Joshua Corbin in 1828) and Benedict Beal.

B. B. Marsh built his home in 1846 and only in recent years was the lovely home torn down. It stood on one of the highest points in Bourbon County where, for more than a century, it overlooked the city of Paris. His birthplace was some distance behind the home he built in 1846.

He was twice married. His first wife was Martha Mitchell, to whom he was married on March 25, 1834. They had one child which lived only a few days. Following the death of his wife Martha in 1836, B. B. Marsh and Martha Jane Ward were married on March 23, 1837. They had seven children—Theodore, Pembrooke, James Nicholas, Eleanor Russell, Beal Crafton, Thomas King and Benedict. It was the dying wish of B. B. Marsh that his son, Benedict, add "Beal" to his name so that he, too, could be known as "B. B."

The Marsh brothers were very excellent silversmiths. In addition, they made beautiful tall case clocks, several of which are still known to exist. The Marsh ledgers were all preserved until a few years ago. The three ledgers remaining contain a wealth of information. One ledger records bets on the Henry Clay election, payable in spoons! B. B. Marsh handled many kinds of merchandise as some of the following items, taken from the Marsh ledgers, will show.

"Everpointed Pencil —	$ 2.50"
"4 Doz. Bullet Buttons—	1.00"
"One Pare Epauletts—	7.00"
"Rep. Fiching Real—	.50"
"One Gold Hart—	1.75"
"Rep. Musical Box—	.50"
"One Gold Fob Chane—	17.00"

1838 MARSH LEDGER

1838 Ledger showing accounts with Benedict Beal Marsh and Thomas King Marsh of Paris. Ledger owned by Miss Jane Marsh.

In 1841 this entry is found:
        "Isaack free man Spear's Boy
May 29   To One Sil. Watch   18.00
        Credt By 37½ gal. whiskey
        at 20 cts. gallon   7.50"

The following account shows one example of the amount of silver often made for a customer:

"1839
4/12—Robert C. Hall—1 Set Tea Spoons   7.50
                                1 Cream Spoon   2.75
                                1 Pare Sug. Tongs   3.50
1840
3/2   1 Soup Spoon   15.00
              1 Set of Desert Spns.   16.00
              1 "   " Tea Spoons   9.00
              1 "   " Table "   26.00"

Another account gives an example of the prices paid for other pieces of silver:

"1838
9/28—Mrs. Abram Spears—
        One Pare Butter Knives   5.00
        One Mustard Spoon   1.00
1841
4/3—Mr. Abram Spears—
        One Pare Butter Knives   6.50
        One Set Table Spoons   25.00
        One Set Desert Spoons   15.00
        One Doz Tea Spoons   17.50
        One Cream Spoon   2.00
        One Pare Sugar Tongs   3.00
        One Castor   20.00"

"Gold specks" were $15.00; one customer paid $9.37½ for 37½ gallons of whiskey which was .25 per gallon; one customer paid $1.50 for "One Gold Button," and another $1.50 for a "Gift Ring." Thomas K. Marsh paid $3.00 cash for "God's Book," while Samuel Clay purchased a "Pare of Specks" for $4.50 and received a .75 credit "By Old Specks," paying $3.75 in cash for the balance. The Marsh brothers mended rings, spoons, "brest" pins, brooches, sugar boxes, etc., and engraved a "Doz. Desert Spoons" for $2.00.

Miss Jane Marsh of Paris, Kentucky, granddaughter of B. B. Marsh, owns the ledgers which are still in existence. She advises she has never seen any silver made by the Marsh brothers marked Flemingsburg. She and her sister own tablespoons made in Richmond by B. B. Marsh, and in addition Miss Marsh owns mustard spoons, tablespoons and a small soup ladle made by her grandfather. Miss Marsh lost by fire several years ago a clock made by Marsh, as well as the cherry table he used as his desk. Mrs. John Pack of Georgetown owns a silver cup made by B. B. Marsh.

In 1844 William M. Hinton became associated with B. B. Marsh to learn the trade of silversmith. When Mr. Marsh retired to the farm in 1854, Mr. Hinton took over the business and became one of the outstanding silversmiths and jewelers of Bourbon and surrounding counties. B. B. Marsh died in 1875 and four years later, in 1879, his wife passed away.

MARSH, THOMAS KING
b. September 13, 1804—Bourbon County
w. Paris

Thomas King Marsh and his brother, Benedict Beal Marsh, were outstanding silversmiths in Paris.

T. K. Marsh was born on September 13, 1804, on his father's farm one mile from Paris. His parents, Beal Marsh and Eleanor Corbin Marsh, were born in Maryland. They had seven children which they raised on the farm near Paris.

In 1831 T. K. Marsh was advertising regularly in the *Western Citizen* of Paris. His brother, B. B. Marsh, learned the silversmith's trade in Philadelphia, after which time he worked in Flemingsburg and Richmond before settling in Paris. The two brothers worked together, making beautiful pieces of silver, handsome tall case clocks and operating a store. They opened their first shop in the neighborhood of the Court House.

Miss Jane Marsh, granddaughter of B. B. Marsh, owns some flat silver and two silver cups made by T. K. Marsh. There are several tall case clocks still in existence which were made by the Marsh brothers, one of which, made by T. K. Marsh, is owned by another descendant. Dr. J. Winston Coleman, Jr., Winburn Farm, Lexington, Kentucky, owns a teaspoon marked "T. K. MARSH" "PARIS, KY."

Many of the old ledgers were lost in a flood some years ago. However, there are still three in existence and they provide a very excellent record of the items sold by the Marsh brothers as well as the silver they made. One ledger records T. K. Marsh's purchase of "God's Book," while another records a bet concerning Henry Clay's election, the bet to be paid in spoons!

T. K. Marsh built his home in Paris in 1847, one year after his brother, B. B. Marsh, had built his new home. In recent years both of these lovely old homes have been torn down.

One source indicates that Thomas K. Marsh married Miss Sallie Wright and moved to Nicholas, thence to Harrison County where he died at an advanced age, although Miss Jane Marsh, a descendant, says that he never married.

MARSHALL, JOHN C.

w. 1836-1849—Louisville

d. 1899—Louisville

John C. Marshall was a silversmith, jeweler and dealer in "fancy goods" in Louisville. From 1836 until 1845 the city directories show that his place of business was located at 15 Main Street between Fourth and Fifth Streets, after which time he was doing business at 467 Main between Fourth and Fifth Streets. In the 1844-45 city directory, under the heading of WATCH, CLOCK, JEWELRY & SILVER SMITHS, the residents of Louisville were advised that "There are several very extensive establishments where these articles are kept in great variety and richness." Included in the list of firms was "J. C. Marshall, south side Main, between Fourth and Fifth." John C. Marshall was interred in Cave Hill Cemetery in Louisville on November 11, 1899.

McCAULLEY, JOHN A.

c. 1840—Richmond

John A. McCaulley was a silversmith of Madison County, working in Richmond. A silver cup, made by this craftsman about 1840, was exhibited at the J. B. Speed Memorial Museum, October Sixth to Twenty-Seventh in 1940, with other silver lent by the Yale University School of Fine Arts from the Mabel Brady Garvan collection.

McCONOTHY, MILTON

w. 1843-1848—Louisville

Milton McConothy was a silversmith who plyed his craft in Louisville. In 1843 he was located on the west side of Fourth Street between Market and Jefferson. In 1848 we find him employed by Richard E. Smith.

McDANNOLD, ————

w. Winchester

No specific dates for this man have been found although it is known that he was a silversmith who worked in Winchester, Clark County. Mrs. Wade Hampton Whitley of Paris, Kentucky, has advised that two silver cups in her family bear the mark of "McDANNOLD." One silver cup is decorated with a beaded border between two narrow borders and is marked simply "McDANNOLD." The second silver cup bears the mark "McDANNOLD" and "PREMIUM."

McGREW AND BEGGS

Louisville probably.

William Beggs, a partner in this firm, was employed by George Griffin in 1838, but nothing has been learned concerning Mr. McGrew. The authors own a butter knife which is marked "McGREW & BEGGS" in a rectangle. It is quite possible that this firm operated in Louisville before 1850.

McMURRAY, THOMAS

w. 1810—Frankfort

Thomas McMurray, a silversmith, advertised in the newspapers of Frankfort in 1810.

MEAD, DANIEL

w. 1845-1848—Louisville

Daniel Mead, a silversmith, first appeared in Louisville in 1845. At that time he was living at 225 Green Street. In 1848 this silversmith was employed at James Fulton's business establishment.

MEDLEY, ANDREW G.

w. 1843-1849—Louisville

Andrew G. Medley was a silversmith, jeweler, watch manufacturer and dealer in "fancy goods" in Louisville. From 1843 until 1845 he was located on the south side of Market between Third and Fourth Streets, where he also lived. Many of the early businessmen found it both convenient and economical to have such an arrangement. By 1846 he had moved to 60 Fourth Street and was boarding at the Exchange Hotel. In the city directory for that year he advertised as follows:

"A. G. MEDLEY,
No. 60 Fourth St., one door from Main,
Dealer In

Jewelry, Silver, Britannia and Plated Ware; Lamps, Knives and Forks, Pen and Pocket Knives, Razors, Scissors, Combs and Brushes, Perfumery, Etc.

Jewelry and Silver Ware made to order in the neatest style. **JEWELRY REPAIRED.**"

He also advertised in the Louisville city directory for 1848-49.

MEEK, BENJAMIN F.

b. September 15, 1816
d. 1901—Louisville
w. 1832-1834—Danville
w. 1834-1882—Frankfort
w. 1882-1901—Louisville

B. F. Meek was a jeweler, watchmaker and a manufacturer of fishing reels. He was born in Mercer County, Kentucky, on September 15, 1816. His parents came from Shadwell, Albemarle County, Virginia, to Mercer County in 1812. B. F. Meek was the youngest of six children, and inherited a fine mechanical skill from his father.

In 1832, at the age of sixteen, B. F. Meek began working with T. R. J. Ayres in Danville, learning the watch repairing and jewelry business. He remained with Mr. Ayres for two years, then returned to Frankfort. The exact year in which he commenced his business is in question. One newspaper of Frankfort advised, in 1877, that B. F. Meek, on Main Street, was organized in 1834, his business consisting of watches, reels and jewelry. Another newspaper of Frankfort had advised two years before that he established his business on Main Street in 1835. In any event, within two or three years after he had returned to Frankfort Benjamin F. Meek entered into partnership with his brother, Jonathan F. Meek, who was seven years his senior. They continued in business together until 1852 when J. F. Meek moved to Louisville and the partnership was dissolved.

On December 28, 1852, *The Commonwealth* of Frankfort carried an advertisement concerning the "New Arrangement," referring to the newly formed partnership of B. F. Meek and B. C. Milam, who proposed to carry on the "Watch, Clock and Jewelry and Reel Business" at the old stand of J. B. Meek and Company on Main Street in Frankfort. In the fall of 1853 the building owned by Meek and Milam was destroyed by fire. The partners rebuilt and occupied the new building during the tenure of the firm. In 1858 the business was divided. B. F. Meek retained the jewelry and watch repairing business which he conducted on the first floor of the building, and B. C. Milam manufactured fishing reels on the second floor. Thus it continued until 1858 when Mr. Meek sold his interest in the building to Dr. Samuel Ayres, a dentist and brother of the silversmith, T. R. J. Ayres.

In 1860 the Kentucky Legislature, by resolution, authorized and directed B. F. Meek to design, as well as make, gold medals for presentation to the surviving soldiers and officers of the Kentucky Volunteers who fought in the battle of Lake Erie on September 10, 1813. The medals were of pure gold, with a circumference of four and seven-eighths inches and weight of thirty-one pennyweights. The obverse side of the medal depicted a naval engagement surrounded by the words, "We have met the enemy and they are ours." The reverse side of the medal was inscribed "To ----- By Resolution of the Kentucky Legislature, February, 1860," enclosed by wreaths of laurel and oak leaves. Four of these medals were made in 1860 and two additional medals were made in 1866.

B. F. Meek advertised in many newspapers of Frankfort. The *Daily Yeoman* in 1865, *The Commonwealth* in 1865 and 1866 as well as the *Semi-Weekly Commonwealth* in 1866, carried the advertisements of B. F. Meek, watchmaker. Mr. Meek's new residence in South Frankfort was described in the *Frankfort Commonwealth* on October 8, 1869. It must have been a lovely residence, for it was brick, two stories in height "after the Gothic style." The *Tri-Weekly Yeoman* of December 19, 1874, carried the advertisement of B. F. Meek, "Watchmaker, Jeweler." Mr. Meek continued his advertising in the *Tri-Weekly Yeoman* during 1876, 1877 and 1878 as a watchmaker and jeweler. In 1881 his advertisement in the *Daily Yeoman* gave his address as the north side of Main Street near the Farmers Bank.

During his many years of business activity in Frankfort, B. F. Meek was active in the political affairs of the city. When North Frankfort and South Frankfort became one corporation in 1880, B. F. Meek was a member of the committee representing South Frankfort which met with the committee for North Frankfort to establish each corporation's share of the existing debts. The two towns had been consolidated in 1850, but property rights were not settled until the Act of 1880.

Late in the year 1882 B. F. Meek left Frankfort, moving to Louisville where he devoted his full time to the manufacture of the fishing reel which made him famous. The *Tri-Weekly Kentucky Yeoman*, in its November 21, 1882, issue, stated that:

> "B. F. MEEK—Frankfort is about to lose one of its oldest and best citizens . . . who, for nearly half a century, has been identified with Frankfort, and by his skill as a maker of fishing reels and repairer of watches has established a reputation co-extensive with the Union. Hereafter he will make his home in Louisville, where he proposes to devote himself to the manufacture of his celebrated fishing reel, for which purpose he has established a suitable shop on the south east corner of Fifth and Jefferson . . ."

B. F. Meek pursued his business activity in Louisville for nine years. He died in 1901.

MEEK, JONATHAN FLEMING

b. 1809
w. 1830-1852—Frankfort
w. 1852-   —Louisville

J. F. Meek was a silversmith, jeweler and manufacturer of fishing reels. In 1812 his parents moved from Shadwell, Albemarle County, Virginia, to Mercer County, Kentucky. J. F. Meek and his brother,

Benjamin F. Meek, were destined to become world-renowned for the fine fishing reels which they made. J. F. Meek did not invent the fishing reel, but he did improve the Snyder reel which was made in 1810.

J. F. Meek had established his jewelry and watch repair business in Frankfort in 1830. He continued alone until he and his brother, Benjamin, formed a partnership in 1837 for the purpose of producing the fishing reels, the sides of which were stamped "J. F. & B. F. MEEK." They continued in business together until 1853 when Jonathan F. Meek moved to Louisville. During the years 1834 and 1835 J. F. Meek was located on the south side of Main Street opposite A. S. Parker's, and advertised in *The Commonwealth* of Frankfort.

The residence of J. F. Meek was located on East Broadway. He sold his home to General John Rodman. Mr. Meek had purchased his property from John J. Vest, the contractor and builder of the house.

J. F. Meek was active in civic affairs, and served as a soldier in the 32nd Kentucky Cavalry, C.S.A.

MEEK, J. F., AND COMPANY

w. 1837-1852—Frankfort

The firm of J. F. Meek and Company was composed of Jonathan Fleming Meek and his brother, Benjamin F. Meek. Their notices in *The Commonwealth* and the *Tri-Weekly Commonwealth* advised the public that they were engaged in the watch, jewelry and reel manufacturing business. The partnership was dissolved when J. F. Meek moved to Louisville in 1852.

MEEK, J. F. AND B. F.

w. 1837-1846—Frankfort

The two Meek brothers, Jonathan Fleming and Benjamin F., were partners in this firm. It would appear from their advertising that they operated under this firm name during the early years of their partnership, for their newspaper advertising from 1841 to 1846 used this firm name. In 1851 and 1852, however, the brothers were advertising in *The Commonwealth* under the name of J. F. Meek and Company. Their business association in Frankfort came to an end in 1852 when J. F. Meek moved to Louisville.

Benjamin Cave Milam had worked with the Meek brothers as an apprentice. When the partnership of J. F. Meek and Company was dissolved in 1852, Benjamin F. Meek and B. C. Milam formed a partnership which continued in operation for five years. Their store on Main Street was destroyed by fire shortly after they began business. The *Tri-Weekly Commonwealth,* on May 1, 1854, carried an article concerning the fire loss and damage in Frankfort's business section, and there we find: "MEEK & MILAM, watchmakers, lost a large portion of their very valuable tools and machinery—no insurance." Following the fire, Meek and Milam located in a small frame building on Lewis Street. Here they remained until they had completed their new building on Main Street. In 1858 B. F. Meek sold his share of the building to Dr. Samuel Ayres of Danville. B. C. Milam continued the manufacture of reels on the second floor.

Some time later B. C. Milam took his son, John W. Milam, into business with him, the firm then becoming B. C. Milam and Son.

MEEK, J. F., B. F. MEEK AND B. C. MILAM
w. 1850-1852—Frankfort

B. C. Milam had worked with the Meek brothers as an apprentice. For a short time the three men were in business together under the firm name of J. F. Meek, B. F. Meek and B. C. Milam. On December 28, 1852, *The Commonwealth* carried the announcement of the dissolution of the copartnership.

MILAM, BENJAMIN CAVE
b. 1821—Frankfort
d. 1904—Frankfort

B. C. Milam was a silversmith, watchmaker and a manufacturer of fishing reels, as well as an able businessman in other fields. He was a Captain in the Mexican War, in command of Company C, First Regiment, Kentucky Mounted Volunteers. In 1847 the town of Frankfort and Franklin County appropriated two hundred dollars each to finance the return of soldiers who fell at Buena Vista. B. C. Milam was chosen to make the trip to Mexico to secure the remains of the men of his company as well as the remains of those who had served under Captain Chambers. The fallen men were buried, with military honors, on September 16, 1847, in the State plot of the Frankfort Cemetery.

B. C. Milam worked for the firm of J. F. and B. F. Meek, learning the business of jeweler, watch repairing and the manufacture of fishing reels. When J. F. Meek left the firm, a new partnership was formed between B. F. Meek and B. C. Milam. They continued in partnership from 1853 until 1858, at which time the business was divided. B. F. Meek continued in the jewelry and watch repair business while B. C. Milam, who thoroughly disliked watch repairing, manufactured reels. Their building was located on Main Street, and Mr. Meek occupied the first floor and Mr. Milam conducted his reel manufactory on the second floor. He taught the business to his son, John W. Milam, and a few years later took him into the business on a partnership basis, the new firm being known as B. C. Milam and Son.

In 1900 B. C. Milam became President of the Deposit Bank in Frankfort, the second man to fill that office. *The Lexington Observer & Reporter* carried the notice of his marriage to Martha Jane Shockley of Frankfort on November 21, 1848. Benjamin C. Milam died in 1904 and was buried in the lovely Frankfort Cemetery just a short distance south of the State Military Monument.

MURRAY, WILLIAM

w. 1850—Louisville

William Murray began business in Louisville in 1850. He came to America from Scotland, and his shop in Louisville was located at 493 Main Street, the "old stand of R. E. Smith." He first advertised in the *Louisville Daily Journal* on July 11, 1850.

NOEL, BEVERLY

w. 1838-1839—Louisville

Beverly Noel was a jeweler who worked for D. C. Fulton, owner of a jewelry and "fancy store" in Louisville.

NOEL, WASHINGTON

w. 1836—Louisville

Washington Noel was a jeweler. His place of business was located on the south side of Main Street, between Third and Fourth Streets. He advertised in the 1836 Louisville city directory as follows:

> "W. NOEL, Dealer in Watches & Jewelry,
> Silver Plate and Britannia Ware,
> Military and Fancy Goods, fine
> Cutlery, etc.
> Fine Watches Repaired.
> South Side of Main, between 3rd
> and 4th streets."

ORR, THOMAS

w. 1848-1849—Louisville

Thomas Orr was a silversmith. In 1848 he was employed by Henry Hudson, but by 1849 he was in business alone as a silversmith and watchmaker on Main Street between Brook and Floyd.

OUTTEN, EPHRIAM

w. 1816-1825—Maysville

d. 1825—Maysville

Ephriam Outten was a silversmith who came to Maysville, Mason County, Kentucky, from Virginia. The exact time of his arrival is not known, but *The Maysville Eagle* of December 24, 1816, carried the announcement that Ephriam Outten was in the house formerly occupied as an office by William B. Phillips.

The Mason County Deed Book R records that on October 13, 1817, George F. Outten was apprenticed to Ephriam Outten of Mason County, Kentucky, to serve for a term of four years from October 1, 1817, to "teach the said George F. Outten the trade and mystery of silversmith."

His parents, Isaac and Margaret Outten, had six children—William, Milky Jones, Mary, Joshua, Jacob and Ephriam. The Mason County Will Book G records the will of Isaac Outten which was dated December 29, 1827, and proven in July Court, 1828.

Other Mason County records show that early in 1822 Ephriam Outten purchased lot No. 110 in the City of Maysville from Joseph McCarty. A mortgage was placed on this property only five years after purchase, and two years after her husband's death, the record states: "Susan Outten, widow of the late Ephriam Outten, deceased, of Maysville, Kentucky, was given clear title to the above mentioned property by the Court."

Ephriam Outten died in 1825. The inventory of his estate lists "bench vices for silversmith," and his will is recorded in Mason County Will Book F. P. H. Baird, another silversmith, was one of the estate appraisers appointed by the court. Administration of the estate was granted to the widow, Susan Outten, and John Griffith.

PARK, JOHN

w. 1848—Louisville

d. 1858—Louisville

John Park was a silversmith in Louisville where, in 1848, he was employed at Henry Hudson's store. He died in 1858. Interment was in Cave Hill Cemetery, October 19, 1858.

PENTECOST, S.

w. 1829—Henderson

S. Pentecost was Henderson County's earliest silversmith. He was advertising in 1829.

PHILLIPS AND FRAZER

w. 1799—Paris

Thomas Phillips was in partnership with Alexander Frazer and Robert Frazer, all three of whom were excellent silversmiths. It is not known when this partnership came into being, but it was dissolved on March 26, 1799. Thomas Phillips continued his business in Paris, while the two Frazer men moved to Lexington to engage in the silversmith business there.

PHILLIPS, THOMAS

w. 1792-1818—Paris

w. 1818-1820—Hopkinsville

w. 1820-1827—Paris

w. 1827-1831—Lawrenceburg

Thomas Phillips was one of Kentucky's earliest silversmiths. He was among the early settlers on, or near, Hardin's Creek in Nelson County. When Washington County was formed from a part of Nelson County in 1792 these settlers became residents of the new county. Thomas Phillips was in partnership with Robert and Alexander Frazer in Paris, Kentucky, and their business covered clock- and watchmaking, jeweler's business and silversmithing. This partnership was dissolved on March 26, 1799, following which the Frazers removed to Lexington, but Thomas Phillips remained in Paris until 1818 when the *Western Citizen* stated he had lately moved to Hopkinsville. He did not remain in Hopkinsville long, for he was advertising in Paris again in 1820 and 1821.

In 1809 Thomas Phillips was located on High Street in Paris, south of the Public Square, between the Presbyterian Church and the home of Hon. Robert Trimble, Judge of the U. S. Supreme Court. The following year Joseph Stephens came to Paris to learn the art of silversmithing from Thomas Phillips. Several years later Mr. Phillips sold his business to Joseph Stephens, at which time he apparently left Paris, for in 1827 Thomas Phillips was granted a license to keep a tavern in Anderson County. He also contributed $10.00 to the Anderson County Court House fund, which was partially financed by popular subscription.

Thomas Phillips and his wife owned a brick tavern on the corner of Woodford and Madison (now Main) Streets in Lawrenceburg which they sold to Matthew Galt for $1,600.

In 1831 Thomas Phillips, who was now a Justice of the Peace, moved out of the state, having spent the preceding few years in Lawrenceburg.

POINDEXTER, WILLIAM A.

b. 1818—Fayette County
d. 1884—Louisville
w. 1838-1859—Lexington

William A. Poindexter was a jeweler, the son of William P. Poindexter, jeweler, who came to Kentucky from Virginia. W. A. Poindexter, one of twelve children, was born in Fayette County in 1818. He never married, but lived at the home of his widowed sister in Lexington. Mr. Poindexter was engaged in the jewelry business for several years, though the exact dates are not known. The Lexington city directory in 1838 tells us that he was in partnership with his father under the firm name of W. Poindexter and Son, while the Lexington city directory in 1859 shows that he was in partnership with C. H. Poindexter under the firm name of C. H. and W. A. Poindexter. They were dealers in watches, jewelry and other allied items and were located on the south side of Main Street between Mill and Upper Streets. William A. Poindexter was interred in the Lexington Cemetery on August 2, 1884.

POINDEXTER, WILLIAM P.

b. 1792—Virginia
d. 1869—Lexington
w. about 1820-1859—Lexington

William P. Poindexter was a jeweler in Lexington for many years. He came to Kentucky from Virginia. At an early age he was apprenticed to a jeweler in Lexington and at the completion of his apprenticeship he opened his own store. When his son, William, was twenty years of age, the father and son formed a partnership under the name of W. Poindexter and Son, and were so carried in the 1838 Lexington city directory.

On February 21, 1846, we find W. P. Poindexter advertising in the *Observer and Reporter:*

"REMOVAL!

WM. POINDEXTER, SR., has Removed his JEWELRY STORE from Main St., to Room number 5, opposite Drs. Whitney and Halstead's Shop, and the 4th down from Norton's Corner or Kennard's Dry Goods Store, between Main and Market streets, where he will be pleased to wait on his old friends and customers, and the public generally."

About 1859 W. P. Poindexter retired to a farm. He had served as a member of the City Council and had sold a tremendous amount of silver which bore his name.

Mr. Poindexter and his wife, Sarah Higbee Poindexter, had twelve children, only seven of whom outlived them. Sarah Poindexter died in 1867 and her husband followed her in death two years later. Both were interred in the Lexington Cemetery—W. P. Poindexter on January 7, 1869, and Sarah on April 10, 1867.

POINDEXTER, W., AND SON

w. 1838-1839—Lexington

This firm is listed in the 1838-39 Lexington city directory as watchmakers and jewelers. Their store was located at 34 West Main Street, and they lived on South Mill Street beyond High and Maxwell.

RAMPP, JOHN

w. 1848-1849—Louisville

John Rampp, a jeweler, is listed in the 1848-49 Louisville city directory. He lived at the home of William Rampp, another Louisville jeweler.

RAMPP, WILLIAM

w. 1848-1859—Louisville

William Rampp was a jeweler who worked in Louisville for about ten years. In 1848 his place of business was located on Jefferson, between Fourth and Fifth Streets, but by 1851 he had moved his store to the north side of Jefferson, between Third and Fourth Streets. He continued to appear in the Louisville city directories until 1859.

REILLY, J. C., AND COMPANY

w. 1816—Louisville

This firm of silversmiths, jewelers, watch- and clockmakers commenced business in Louisville on March 20, 1816. Miss Mary Verhoeff, Vice-President of The Filson Club in Louisville owns a complete file of *The Western Courier* newspapers, and with her permission the following advertisement from the May 9, 1816, *Western Courier* is used:

"J. C. REILLY & COMPANY
WATCH & CLOCK-MAKERS,
SILVERSMITHS AND JEWELLERS,

Respectfully inform their friends and the public in general, that they have commenced the above business in all its various branches, in the shop lately occupied by Messrs. Blanton and Larkin, the next door to William Anderson's & Co's. store, where they hope, by their unremitted attention to business, to share a part of the public patronage.

Clocks And Watches of every description made and repaired, and warrented to perform. They have on hand, and intend keeping a large and general assortment of *Silver-Work And Jewellery* in all of the best quality, and neatest fashion:

N.B. *Two Or Three Journeymen* at the above business, will meet with constant employment.

Wanted also, Two or Three *Apprentices* at the above business...Boys of good moral characters."

RICHARDSON, GEORGE

w. 1845-1848—Louisville

George Richardson was a silver plater. During 1845 and 1846 he was located at 597 Main Street, and in 1848 he was employed by Robert Steele.

RIGGS, BENJAMIN McKENNY

b. 1799—Maryland
d. November 18, 1839—Paris
w. Prior to 1825-1839—Paris

B. M. Riggs was a silversmith who worked in Paris, Kentucky. He was born in Maryland in 1799, and came to Kentucky before 1825. He worked at his trade in Paris until his death on November 18, 1839. His residence was on Pleasant Street in Paris. On July 12, 1831, B. M. Riggs advertised in *The Western Citizen* for an apprentice. A member of Mrs. Wade Hampton Whitley's family owns spoons made by B. M. Riggs before 1833.

RIGGS, DAVID H.

w. 1840–Paris

David H. Riggs was another of Bourbon County's excellent silversmiths. He was probably the son of Benjamin McKenny Riggs. On February 28, 1840, Mr. Riggs advised the public he "intends to manufacture spoons in the shop of Geo. Snyder on Main Street some doors above Talbott's Hotel," and asks the public's patronage.

ROBERTS, JAMES S. H.

w. 1806–Lexington

w. 1807–Frankfort

James S. H. Roberts was a silversmith who made his first appearance in Lexington in 1806. He advertised in the November 17, 1806, *Kentucky Gazette* as a silversmith, goldsmith and jeweler. On November 12, 1807, the *Western World* of Frankfort contained the advertisement of James S. H. Roberts, gold- and silversmith, who had "lately opened a shop in Frankfort." He was the son of P. D. Roberts, a Frenchman.

SAVAGE, WILLIAM M.

w. 1805-1820–Glasgow

William M. Savage was probably the outstanding silversmith of Barren County. The marriage records of Barren County show his marriage, in 1805, to Susanna Williams. He came to Glasgow shortly after the turn of the century, where he worked as a silversmith and watchmaker. Following his retirement as a silversmith he kept a tavern and operated a cotton gin. The firm of Eubank and Jeffries succeeded him in business.

SAVAGE AND EUBANK

c. 1805-1820–Glasgow

William M. Savage and James Eubank were partners for an undetermined period between 1805 and 1820. In 1820 W. M. Savage retired from the business of silversmith and was succeeded by Eubank and Jeffries. Apparently the firm of Savage and Eubank was in existence during William M. Savage's early years in Glasgow.

DAVID A. SAYRE

Portrait hangs at Sayre School, Lexington, which was founded by David A. Sayre in 1854. Year-long celebration of the school's centennial in 1954.

SAYRE, DAVID A.

b. March 12, 1793—Madison, New Jersey
d. September 12, 1870—Lexington
w. 1811-1829—Lexington

David A. Sayre was a silversmith, banker and philanthropist. Born in Madison, New Jersey, on March 12, 1793, he came to Kentucky while still quite young. In 1811 he came to Lexington from Maysville, without funds. He had acquired a knowledge of the silversmith's art and was employed for a time by Ezra Woodruff in Lexington. He worked hard, was thrifty, and his business prospered. On August 18, 1825, he and Miss Abby V. Hammond were married in the Lexington Episcopal Church. No children were born to this marriage, but he later took his nephew, Ephraim Sayre, into the banking business with him. In 1823 David Sayre had added a brokerage office to his regular business of silversmith, and five years later, in 1829, he was engaged solely in the banking business which he established at the northeast corner of Mill and Short Streets.

David A. Sayre became a very wealthy man. He was a member of the Presbyterian Church, assisted in the raising of funds to purchase land for a cemetery and served as one of the original incorporators of the cemetery which was dedicated June 25, 1850. He financed the education of many young people, was the first Treasurer of the Kentucky Agricultural and Mechanical Association which was incorporated on December 7, 1850 and, perhaps as his greatest living contribution to the community, established the Sayre Female Institute for which, in 1854, he donated the grounds and fine buildings, and during his lifetime added generously to his original gift. David A. Sayre also served as one of the appraisers of the estate of Edward West, silversmith.

Mr. Sayre died September 12, 1870. He and his wife, who was affectionately known as "Aunt Abby," are interred in the Lexington Cemetery.

SAYRE, L.

Probably Lexington

Spoons bearing the mark of L. Sayre are in existence, although it has not been learned whether he was actually a silversmith, or whether he was a jeweler.

SCHWING, JOHN G.

b. 1783—Strasbourg, Germany
d. 1868—Louisville
w. 1803 to about 1820—Louisville

John G. Schwing was a goldsmith and jeweler. The son of Johann G. Schwing, a watchmaker from Strasbourg, Germany, who came to America before the Revolutionary War, John G. Schwing came to Louisville in 1803. The *Farmers Library and Ohio Intelligencer* of March 10, 1803, carried his advertisement which read: "John G. Schwing, Goldsmith, Jeweler, respectfully informs citizens of Louisville, that he has commenced business."

He married Miss Mary Kaye in 1812. A daughter, Maria, married William Kendrick on January 19, 1832, thereby relating two families who were to be well remembered in the silver and jewelry business. In 1832 J. G. Schwing built a home on the northwest corner of Seventh and Walnut, and shortly after that William Kendrick and his bride built their lovely brick residence nearby.

John G. Schwing remained in the silversmith and jeweler's business for only a few years, for we find he was the first man in Louisville to apply steam to machinery. He built a sawmill, about 1830 he built a gristmill in the locality of Old Frankfort Avenue, and finally a flourmill which could manufacture fifty barrels of flour a day.

By 1860 Mr. Schwing's son-in-law, William Kendrick, had built a larger home to accommodate "Grandfather" and "Grandmother" Schwing in addition to his five daughters, two sons, himself and his wife. John G. Schwing died in Louisville in 1868.

SCOTT AND KITTS

w. 1843-1845—Louisville

The firm of Scott and Kitts is listed in the 1843-44 Louisville city directory. They conducted a "fancy and jewellers store" on the northwest corner of Main and Wall Streets. William D. Scott and John Kitts formed their partnership in 1843, but less than two years later the partnership was dissolved. Both W. D. Scott and John Kitts were advertising alone in 1845.

SCOTT, WILLIAM D.

w. 1841-1849—Louisville

William D. Scott was a jeweler and watchmaker. In 1841 he was employed at Richard E. Smith's store. In 1843 he formed a partnership with John Kitts. This partnership lasted less than two years, for by the latter part of 1844 William D. Scott was working alone at the northwest corner of Main and Wall Streets and had employed T. M. Scott, a watchmaker.

The 1844-45 Louisville city directory contained the following advertisement for W. D. Scott:

"W. D. SCOTT
N. W. Cor. Wall and Main Streets
Dealer In

Watches, Jewelry, Fine Cutlery, Silver
And Plated Ware
Military and Fancy Goods,
Lamps, Etc.

Watches & Jewelry repaired in the best manner."

In 1845 W. D. Scott moved his jewelry store to 496 Main Street, and in 1848 he was located at 489 Main Street, between Third and Fourth Streets. He had also added another employee, William Messick. During 1848 his firm became W. D. Scott and Company.

SCOTT, W. D., AND COMPANY
w. 1848-1849—Louisville

This firm was organized in 1848, but was short-lived, continuing in business approximately one year.

SCOTTHORN, ————
w. 1799—Shelby County

A silversmith whose last name was Scotthorn was Shelby County's earliest craftsman. Mr. Absalom Matthews of Shelby County, Kentucky, received a letter, dated December 7, 1872, from John W. Williamson, of O'Bannon Station, Jefferson County, Kentucky, in which he mentions a Mr. Scotthorn, silversmith, working in Shelby County in 1799.

SHARP, GEORGE
w. 1850-1870—Danville

George Sharp was a silversmith who worked in Danville. Just when he began work as a silversmith is not known, but after T. R. J. Ayres, silversmith, left Danville, George Sharp continued with the business, marking his silver "G. SHARP." He made quite a number of silver cups.

SHARRARD, JAMES S.

w. 1836—Scott County
w. 1841—Paris
w. 1842-1861—Shelbyville
    Henderson
    Owensboro
    Paducah

James S. Sharrard was an itinerant silversmith for many years, traveling through the countryside making lovely pieces of silver from the coins which had been saved for that purpose. His son, Judson Sharrard, also was a silversmith, as was his brother-in-law, Warren B. Ewing. His brother, William M. Sharrard, is also known to have been a silversmith. Since it is known that J. S. Sharrard worked in many cities, it is possible that, with the aid of his brother, son and son-in-law, shops were maintained in more than one city at one time.

In 1847 his shop in Shelbyville was located opposite the Post Office, on Main Street, and he worked in Shelbyville longer than in any other place. Early in the 1840's Warren B. Ewing came to Shelbyville from Paris, at which time he went into business with James S. Sharrard. It has not been learned how long this partnership lasted.

SHARRARD AND EWING

w. Early 1840's—Shelbyville

Warren B. Ewing came to Shelbyville from Paris to join his brother-in-law, James S. Sharrard, in the silversmithing business. Both men were silversmiths. It has not been determined how long the partnership endured.

SHARRARD, JUDSON

c. 1850

Judson Sharrard, the son of James S. Sharrard, was a silversmith. The locality in which he worked is not known, nor do we know when he worked. However, in view of the fact that his father was, for many years, an itinerant silversmith who worked in Scott County, Paris, Shelbyville, Henderson, Owensboro, Harrodsburg and Paducah, it is quite possible that they maintained a place of business in more than one city at a time.

SHARRARD, WILLIAM M.

c. 1839-1850

William M. Sharrard, silversmith, was a brother of James S. Sharrard, an itinerant silversmith, who worked in many cities through the years. It seems reasonable to assume that this family of silversmiths operated in more than one city at a time. One source has placed William M. Sharrard in Harrodsburg, but nothing definite has been found to establish when and where he worked. He and Elizabeth Beatty of Georgetown were married in 1839.

SHEPARD, ALPHEUS XAVIER FRANCIS

b. October, 1795—Georgetown

w. About 1815-1831—Georgetown

A. X. F. Shepard was one of Scott County's first silversmiths. He had several apprentices and produced a large amount of beautiful silver. His father, Samuel Shepard, was born in New Middlesex County, Massachusetts, in 1765 and came to Kentucky before it was yet a state. He settled in Georgetown, where he opened the town's first tavern. On March 27, 1792, he and Miss Frankie Barlow were married in Georgetown. Samuel Shepard was a pioneer lawyer and surveyor, a justice of the peace, chairman of the Georgetown Board of Trustees, represented Scott County in the State Legislature in 1816, drew up the plans for the jail in 1804, and served as jailor in 1807. Four sons and one daughter were born to Samuel and Frankie Shepard. The daughter died at the age of twelve, but the sons grew to manhood and became well known citizens. James Madison, the youngest son, born in 1802, never married. He served in the Kentucky Legislature as a Senator in 1850-51, was a Circuit Court Judge in 1857, and served in the Civil War as First Lieutenant in the Federal Cavalry Company organized by Dr. S. F. Gano of Georgetown.

In 1817 Thomas Jefferson Shepard, aged sixteen, began his apprenticeship under his brother, A. X. F. Shepard. In 1831 A. X. F. Shepard sold his jewelry store in Georgetown to his brother, Thomas Jefferson Shepard.

SHEPARD, THOMAS JEFFERSON

b. January 15, 1801—Georgetown

d. February, 1875—Georgetown

w. 1817-1828—Georgetown

w. 1828-1831—Louisville

w. 1831-1875—Georgetown

Thomas Jefferson Shepard was a silversmith who learned the trade in Georgetown as an apprentice to his brother, A. X. F. Shepard. His father, Samuel Shepard, born in New Middlesex County, Massachusetts, in 1765, came to Kentucky before it was made a state. He settled in Georgetown where, on March 27, 1792, he married Miss Frankie Barlow. They had five children—four sons and one daughter. Two of the sons, Alpheus Xavier Francis and Thomas Jefferson, were to become outstanding silversmiths.

In 1817, at the age of sixteen, Thomas Jefferson Shepard commenced his apprenticeship under his brother. In 1828 T. J. Shepard went to Louisville, where he was employed by Beard and Ayres until 1831, when he returned to Georgetown. Upon his return, T. J. Shepard purchased the jewelry store which had been owned and operated by his brother, A. X. F. Shepard, for many years. From that time until his death in 1875 he carried on his business in Georgetown.

T. J. Shepard was twice married. He married Miss Amanda Smith of Scott County in November, 1830. Three children were born of this marriage. In 1852 he married Mrs. Eliza (Woodruff) Morford, and two sons were born of this marriage. A resident of Georgetown owns a cup bearing the mark of "T. J. SHEPARD" "GEORGETOWN, KY."

SHEPHERD, EPHRAIM

w. 1834-1836—Newport

Ephraim Shepherd was a silversmith who worked in Newport, Kentucky, from 1834 until 1836. He moved from Newport to Cincinnati, Ohio.

SIMPKINS, JAMES

w. 1845-1846—Louisville

The 1845-46 Louisville city directory lists James Simpkins as a silverplate worker at 597 Main Street.

SIMPSON, JONATHAN

w. prior to 1830-1861—Bardstown
1861-1863—Madison, Indiana
1863—Bardstown
d. 1863—Bardstown

Jonathan Simpson, silversmith, appears to have been in Nelson County before 1820, and to have been working there shortly thereafter. He resided in the Heavenhill homestead near Bardstown. He was not only an excellent silversmith, but made clocks and repaired surveying instruments as well.

About 1861 Jonathan Simpson moved to Madison, Jefferson County, Indiana, but returned to Bardstown, Kentucky, in 1863. He owned property in both Madison, Indiana, and Bardstown, Kentucky. Upon his death in 1863 his executor, William H. Keyt, made application to the "Fifth Judicial Court of Common Please," Jefferson County, Indiana, December 26, 1863, for "Letters Testamentary" in the matter of the estate of Jonathan Simpson, Deceased, swearing "that the personal property of Jonathan Simpson, deceased," was "not worth over Six hundred and real estate directed by the will to be sold does not exceed in Value the sum of Two thousand dollars, As I believe so help me God."

Nelson County Will Record Book 12 records the will of Jonathan Simpson as follows:

> "Know all men by these presents, that I Jonathan Simpson for a year or two back a resident of the City of Madison Ind^a but designing hereafter to reside in Nelson County Kentucky; which was for many years my former home, having in view the uncertainty of life and wishing while in health to dispose of my woldly effect, do make and declare the following as my last will and Testament, for the disposition of all my property both real and personal; both in Kentucky and Indiana—
>
> My will for the disposition of all my property after my decease is as follows—To Wit:
>
> Item 1st I do hereby bequeath to my Grand Son John Desha Simpson; son of my own son James Simpson now of the State of Texas, the sum of One Thousand Dollars to be paid to him by my Executor with interest thereon from the time of my decease, when he shall arrive at the age of twenty one years. This bequest of One Thousand Dollars as above, is given however with this express condition, that it is and shall be in full of all claim—that may arise against my estate in consequence of a Note executed by me to John W. G. Simrall as guardian of said John Desha Simpson; for the sum of One Hundred and Fifteen Dollars Fifty five cents, executed by me in Louisville Ky. November 3rd 1853 payable Twelve Months after date with interest from the 30th day of September 1853—
>
> Item 2nd In the event of the death of my said Grand son John Desha Simpson before he shall arrive at the age of Twenty one years as above or before he shall receive said sum above bequeathed to him—I hereby give said Thousand Dollars with the interest to my daughter Mary M. Jones now of Madison Indiana and to my son James Simpson now of Texas to be divided equally between them.
>
> Item 3rd All the remaining portion of my property both real and personal in Kentucky and Indiana. I hereby authorize and require my Executor (who is hereafter named) to sell and dispose of to the best advantage in his power—to be divided equally between my daughter Mary M. Jones—and my son James Simpson as aforesaid—
>
> The sale and division to be made as promptly as practicable—without sacrifice of the property—which my said Executor is authorized to sell for cash in hand

or on credit at his discretion—

Item 4th I do hereby appoint William H. Keyt—now of Madison, Indiana as my Executor of my last will will and Testament, with full power and authority to sell an convey Real Estate both in Kentucky and Indiana—and with all power necessary fully to execute and carry out my Will as expressed above—

    Whereof witness my hand seal this 10th day of April A.D. 1863 in the City of Madison Jefferson County State of Indiana.

        JONATHAN SIMPSON

We the undersigned at the request of Jonathan Simpson the above named Testator, attest the signing of the foregoing writing, written on an half sheet of paper which we do in the presence of the testator and in the presence of each other and the said Simpson acknowledged the above as his last will and testament and request us to attest the same as such.

      EDWIN G. LELAND
      LUTHER G. WEST"

The unusual spelling of some words and the lack of punctuation have been reproduced as the will was recorded.

Jonathan Simpson is known to have made tablespoons, teaspoons, dessert spoons, ladles and silver cups.

SMART, GEORGE

w. 1794—Lexington

George Smart was a silversmith who came to America from England, arriving in Lexington in 1794.

SMITH, GEORGE E.

w. 1848-1849—Louisville

The Louisville city directories for 1848 and 1848-49 list George E. Smith, a watchmaker and jeweler, living at 494 Broadway, between First and Second Streets.

SMITH AND GRANT

w. 1827-1831—Louisville

The firm of Smith and Grant was advertising its jewelry business in 1827, but on November 10, 1831, the *Louisville Daily Journal* carried a notice that "The co-partnership of Smith and Grant was dissolved by mutual consent on the 26th of August last . . ." Richard Ewing Smith of this firm had come to Louisville from Windsor, Vermont, about 1821.

SMITH, J. W. W.

w. 1847—Shelbyville

J. W. W. Smith advertised the opening of his shop on Main Street in Shelbyville on March 17, 1847. It is not known how long this silversmith worked in Shelbyville.

SMITH AND KITTS

w. 1844-1845—Louisville

The 1844-45 Louisville city directory lists John Kitts, of the firm of Smith and Kitts. No other information has been found concerning this partnership.

SMITH, RICHARD EWING

b. 1800

d. 1849—Louisville

w. 1821-1849—Louisville

Richard Ewing Smith came to Louisville from Windsor, Vermont, about 1821. He opened a jewelry store on Main Street, where he continued in business until his death in 1849.

In 1827 R. E. Smith formed a partnership with a Mr. Grant which endured for five years. November 10, 1831, the *Louisville Daily Journal* advised "The Co-partnership of Smith and Grant was dissolved by mutual consent on the 26th of August last . . . and will be continued by Richard E. Smith."

R. E. Smith was a progressive businessman. He made a trip to New York for the express purpose of securing the services of several skilled silversmiths whom he brought back to Louisville with him. The firm then placed on the market in Louisville silver forks and other items which were made at Mr. Smith's shop.

From 1832 until 1846 R. E. Smith was located on the south side of Main near Fourth Street, according to the directories. By 1846 his address is "493 Main Street"; although his shop location had been given a number, it was still the same spot in which he had originally opened his business. He had many employees through the years. Peter Daumont, Mr. Harris, Edgar S. Wait and John F. Wright, jewelers; George Modeman, William Scott, watchmakers, and Milton McConothy, a silversmith, were among those employed by him. The 1844 Louisville city directory lists Richard Ewing Smith under the heading of "Watch, Clock, Jewelry and Silver Smiths." At that time he carried a "rich and varied stock."

He married Catharine Hays, who died in March, 1893, at the age of ninety-two, in Paducah, Kentucky. Their first-born, Sophie, married Adam Rankin who opened the Branch Bank of Louisville in Paducah. R. E. Smith was probably the grandson of Steel Smith who was born in 1729 or 1730, and who died on April 5, 1812.

SMITH, THOMAS

    b. November 22, 1790—Henry County

    d. August 7, 1850

    w. 1818—Lexington

Thomas Smith appears in the 1818 Lexington city directory as a silversmith. His father, Nicholas Smith, came to Henry County, Kentucky, from Virginia, and settled about five miles southeast of New Castle, Henry County, Kentucky. Thomas Smith, born November 22, 1790, was well educated, and after reaching manhood left his father's farm in which he had no interest. He began his business career in Shelbyville, working in a store, but before long he and Captain Searny had established a business at Old Port William. Some time later he moved to New Castle, Henry County, where he was associated with his brother, William Smith, and Daniel Brannin.

Proof of his financial success is evidenced by the fact that in 1837 his wealth was more than one-half million dollars. In 1837 he disposed of his mercantile business interests in order to devote his full time to the management and increase of his estate. From 1847 until his death in 1850 he served as President of the Louisville and Frankfort Railroad, which was under construction at that time.

Thomas Smith married Harriet Owens, the daughter of Colonel Abram Owens, who was an officer in the War of 1812. They reared a family of seven children.

SMITH, W. C.

    Bowling Green

Little is known of this craftsman. W. C. Smith was a silversmith who made, among other things, lovely silver cups. One source places him in Bowling Green from 1850 to 1860. There was also a William C. Smith of Lincoln County who was a taxpayer in 1790, but no proof is found that this man and the silversmith of Bowling Green were the same person.

SNYDER, GEORGE W., JR.

    w. 1821-1848—Paris

George W. Snyder, Jr., and George W. Snyder, Sr., were silversmiths who worked in Paris, Kentucky. In 1821 Snyder's shop was mentioned in the advertisement of a Mr. Hughes, cabinet maker, who was located opposite Lyon's Tavern. On May 20, 1831, shortly after the death of his wife, G. W. Snyder, Jr., advertised he had decided to quit the silversmith business. He later was in business of another kind which he conducted in the same shop where he had followed the trade of silversmith, although from 1845 until 1848 he and his son, James C. Snyder, were partners in the silversmithing business.

Mrs. Wade Hampton Whitley of Paris advises he was buried in the cemetery on Stoner Avenue in Paris, near the present intersection of Massie and Maysville Streets. More than forty years ago Mrs. Whitley had copied the name from the old stone in the abandoned cemetery. Few of the inscriptions were legible, but the name of George W. Snyder, Jr., could be read.

Mrs. Whitley has in her possession the original bill which was rendered to a third great-uncle, Mr. Thomas Stamps, by George W. Snyder, Jr., in 1826:

"1826
Feb. 15th	To one Gold Leaver watch & Riggin
Mar. 10th	To Cleaning a gold watch and repairs
July 21st	One pair of Silver Specks
Dec. 4th	To one Gold finger Ring
Feb. 15th	Credit by Cash $100
J...... 16th	Credit by Cash $ 60
Aug. 12	Credit by 22 Bushels of apples
Aug. 20	" " 20 loads of wood
Aug. 20	" " 416 lbs. of pork

Balance due $25.84½"

An old family account book of 1826 owned by Mrs. Whitley gives the price of apples .25 per bushel, wood $1.25 per load and pork a little less than .02½ per pound, since on December 13, 1826, Mr. Stamps sold 346 pounds of pork for $7.87½. The total of cash paid, plus the value of the merchandise for which he was given credit, plus the $25.84½ balance due, would certainly indicate that the gold watch was a rather expensive one!

SNYDER, GEORGE W., SR.

w. 1803-1813—Paris

d. 1813—Paris

George W. Snyder, Sr., was a watchmaker, silversmith and inventor. His son, George W. Snyder, Jr., was also a silversmith.

G. W. Snyder, Sr., came to Kentucky from Pennsylvania in 1803, and settled in Hopewell (Paris). Sarah Snyder Wakefield of Norfolk, Virginia, a descendant, advises that he was born in Germany, where he learned his trade. In 1810 he built the Kentucky reel, the first multiplying reel in the world, and served as President of the Bourbon

County Anglers Association. Benjamin and Jonathan Meek, as well as Benjamin Milam, improved the reel invented by Snyder, but George W. Snyder, Sr., was the inventor.

On September 1, 1813, he advertised in the *Western Citizen* of Paris that he had opened a watch business two doors below the Post Office, and further advised the public he wanted to buy old brass. He died later this same year.

Mrs. Whitley of Paris, Kentucky, owns a ladle which was made by this silversmith marked "G S" in one stamp, and "PARIS" in another. The ladle was a wedding gift to an aunt of many generations ago who was married before 1815 and who died during the cholera epidemic of 1833. Mrs. Whitley writes: "These big old ladles were always used as skimmers at preserving and jelly-making time in our family." Mrs. Wakefield advises the Snyders also made grandfather clocks with wooden works, and that several of these clocks are owned by persons living in central Kentucky.

SNYDER, JAMES C.

b. 1815

d. September 16, 1852—Paris

w. 1845-1852—Paris

James C. Snyder, silversmith, was the son of G. W. Snyder, Jr., silversmith, and the grandson of G. W. Snyder, Sr., also a silversmith. His mother was Catherine Snyder.

He was in partnership with his father from 1845 until 1848, but worked alone from 1848 until his death in 1852. James C. Snyder was born in 1815. In 1843 he married Elizabeth Ann Reynolds (born 1826). Three children were born of this marriage—George Reynolds, Robert J., and Charlie.

SNYDER, J. C. AND G. W.

w. 1845-1848—Paris

The firm of J. C. and G. W. Snyder, silversmiths, was a partnership between James C. Snyder and his father, George W. Snyder, Jr.

SPEARS, DAVID H.

Springfield prior to 1850

It has been said that David H. Spears was a silversmith in Springfield before 1850. The authors have not been able to establish proof of the fact he worked in Springfield, but they have seen silver made by him.

SPEIGELHALDER, FERDINAND

w. 1836-1867—Louisville

From 1836 until 1867 Ferdinand Speigelhalder was a member of the Louisville firm of Speigelhalder and Werne, jewelers.

SPEIGELHALDER, JOHN F.

w. 1844-1867—Louisville

John Speigelhalder was listed with the firm of Speigelhalder and Werne in the 1844-45 Louisville city directory, and as a member of the firm of Speigelhalder and Sons from 1865 to 1867.

SPEIGELHALDER AND WERNE

w. 1836-1858—Louisville

Ferdinand Speigelhalder and Joseph Werne, Sr., were partners in this firm of clock- and watchmakers and jewelers. They began their business on the west side of Fifth Street between Main and Market Streets where they continued until 1845 when they moved to the west side of Third between Market and Jefferson Streets. The 1844-45 Louisville city directory carried the following advertisement for the firm:

"SPEIGELHALDER & WERNE

Dealers In

WATCHES & CLOCKS

Jewelry, Silverware, Etc.

No. 82, 3d, between Market and Jeff. sts.,

Clocks and Watches Repaired and Warranted."

The 1848 Louisville city directory carried the same advertisement for this firm. They continued in business at 82 Third Street, between Market and Jefferson until the death of Mr. Werne in 1858, at which time the firm became known as Speigelhalder and Sons. The directories do not carry the spelling of "Speigelhalder" consistently, being frequently spelled "Spiegelhalder." The use of the first spelling has been given here throughout.

SPURGIN, DAVID M.

b. 1814—Mt. Sterling
w. 1829—Mt. Sterling
w.   —Winchester
w. 1833-1847—Carlisle
w. 1847-1852—Winchester
   1852   —Indiana

David M. Spurgin was a silversmith who worked in many places during his twenty-three years of business activity in Kentucky. He was born May 7, 1814, at Mt. Sterling, where, at the age of fifteen he began his apprenticeship with Samuel Hensley, a silversmith. He did not serve the full seven years as an apprentice, for we learn that he worked as a journeyman for Smith Jeffries in Winchester following his training with Mr. Hensley, later buying Mr. Hensley's business in its entirety in 1833. He moved the newly acquired silversmith business from Mt. Sterling to Carlisle on June 14, 1833, continuing there until 1847, at which time he moved to Winchester. He worked as a silver craftsman in Winchester until he moved to Greencastle, Indiana, in 1852.

STEELE, ROBERT

w. 1832-1848—Louisville

Robert Steele was a silver plater who worked in Louisville. He appears first in the 1832 Louisville city directory, at which time he was working on Third Street near Main. Sometime between 1832 and 1838 he moved to Main Street between Brook and Floyd Streets, where he continued in business until 1844. For about a year his shop was on Third Street between Walnut and Chestnut, but in 1845 he moved his business to 648 Main. He lived at the shop until 1845 when he changed his residence to 133 Second Street. In 1848 he was living on Main Street between Hancock and Clay. George Richardson, a silver plater, was employed by Mr. Steele in 1848.

Fayette County Will Book B records the will of Richard Steele. The will was written November 15, 1808, probated in May, 1809, and names his wife, Martha, five sons, Adam, Richard, Joseph, John and Robert M., and two daughters Polly Sutherland and Patsy Beal.

STEELE, REV. WILLIAM

1780-1844

William Steele was a Christian minister as well as an early craftsman. He and his family came to Kentucky from Pennsylvania in 1780 with a company under the direction of Houston and Miller. There were thirty-three boats and canoes which started from Wheeling, traveling down the Ohio River to Kentucky. Four of the boats landed at Limestone (Maysville), the others continuing to the Falls of the Ohio (Louisville). In a deposition filed in Bourbon County William Steele stated that he, together with others of their company, came to Ruddles' Station six or seven miles below the improvement of John Miller, going thence to Martin's Station about six or seven miles from Miller's improvement to secure men to guard their families on the trip from Limestone (Maysville) to the lots they had drawn. They secured the services of only fourteen men from these two stations, and on the return trip to Limestone the Indians stole about twenty horses from them, making it impossible for their families to be moved safely. The party then returned to the Falls of Ohio for safety, where in 1780 William Steele met John Miller and his family. The following winter Rev. Steele and Mr. Miller arrived at the lots they had previously drawn. William Steele, Jr., a nephew of the minister, was one of the group of new settlers.

William Steele was one of the soldiers of the American Revolution honored by a D.A.R. tablet which was unveiled on Saturday, June 4, 1927, in Paris, Kentucky. The *First Census of Kentucky* lists William Steele, under date of November 29, 1789, as a taxpayer in Fayette County.

STEELE AND CARR

w. 1836–Louisville

The firm of Steele and Carr appeared in the 1836 Louisville city directory as "coach silverplaters." They placed an advertisement in this directory which read:

> "**STEELE & CARR,** Coach & Harness Makers and Silver Platers, Main street, Louisville, Ky. Steele & Carr are engaged in the above business in all its various branches, etc."

STEPHENS, JOSEPH LAWRENCE

b. April 17, 1764–Frederick County, Virginia
d. February 14, 1848
w. 1810-1827–Paris

J. L. Stephens was a silversmith. He came to Paris in 1810, where he learned the art of silversmithing from Thomas Phillips whom he succeeded in business several years later. It appears he did not carry on the silversmithing business for long after succeeding Thomas Phillips.

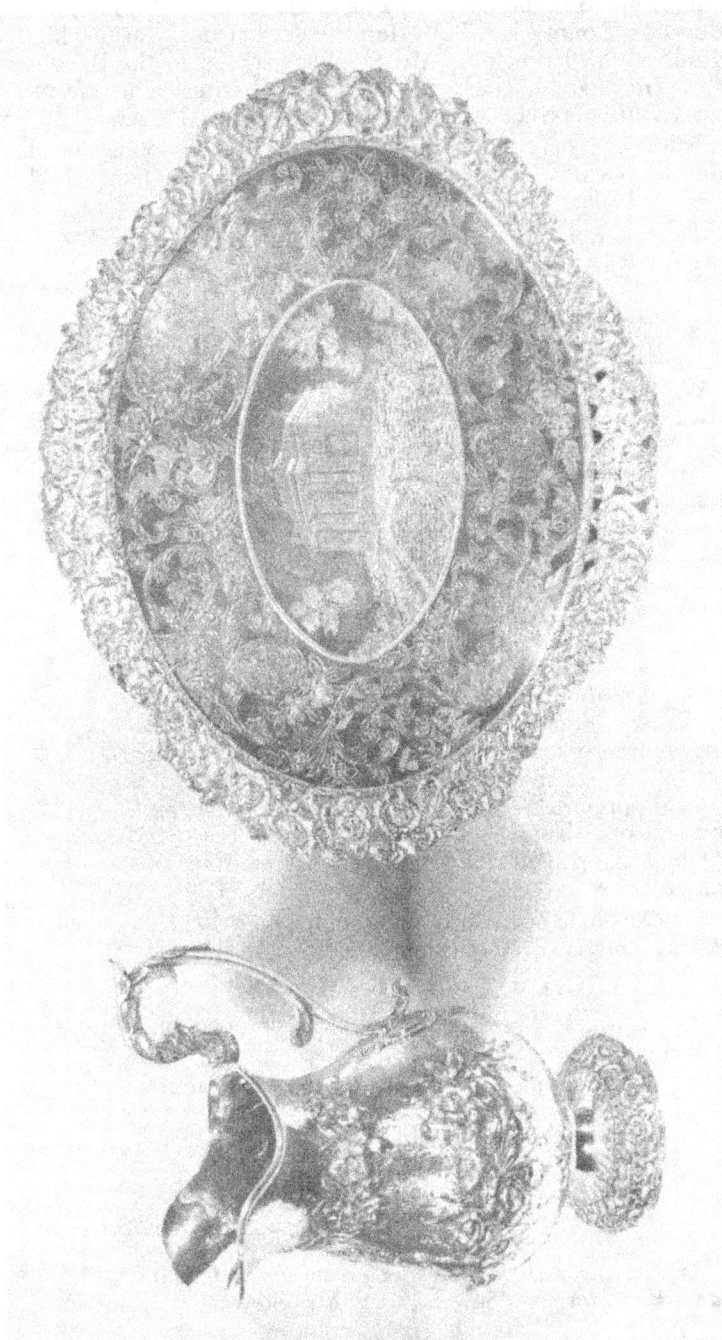

STEWART PITCHER AND TRAY

Silver Pitcher and Tray made by George W. Stewart, Lexington. Owned by the Victor Bogaert Jewelry Company, formerly belonging to Charles J. Flournoy of Fayette County.

He was born on April 17, 1764, in Frederick County, Virginia, and came to Bourbon County in 1789. Here he settled on a farm which adjoined Ruddle's Mill precinct. Mr. Stephens served in the Revolutionary War. He died February 14, 1848, and was buried in the old cemetery at Cynthiana. His wife lived but two years longer.

There are many spoons and some silver cups to be found which were made by Joseph Lawrence Stephens, which are marked "J. STEPHENS" "PARIS."

STEWART, GEORGE W.
w. 1846-1852—Lexington

George W. Stewart was an excellent silversmith. He made exquisite flatware, as well as silver cups, pitchers, trays and tea sets. Thomas G. Calvert, who was to become one of Lexington's leading jewelers, learned the trade under G. W. Stewart and later bought his business.

The *Observer and Reporter* of Lexington, on April 4, 1846, carried the following advertisement:

"SILVER FORKS!
TEA SETS, ETC.

The subscriber has on hand and is manufacturing Forks and Spoons of new and beautiful patterns, and guarantees the silver to be equal to the French and Spanish standard, which he will sell as low as can be purchased in the Eastern cities, of the same quality of silver. Also manufacturing Tea Sets, Pitchers, Cups, etc. of the best workmanship and patterns.

I have on hand a fine assortment genuine M. I. Tobia's and Wm. Robinson's make of

GOLD WATCHES

Which I will sell low, and warrant to be good time keepers.

Strict attention paid to the Repairing of Watches.

* * Every description of ENGRAVING neatly executed.

GEO. W. STEWART
No. 1 Cheapside, Lex."

In 1846 Mr. Stewart's store was located at No. 1 Cheapside. The *Observer and Reporter*, in 1847, advised Mr. Stewart was at No. 2 Cheapside.

STEWART, WILLIAM

w. 1790-1851—Russellville

d. 1874—Jessamine County

William Stewart was one of Kentucky's earliest silversmiths. The *First Census of Kentucky* lists William Stewart as a taxpayer—one entry dated January 11, 1790, and another under date of July 23, 1790. The same year he arrived in Russellville where he carried on his trade of silversmith. Apparently he remained there until about 1851. He was living in Jessamine County at the time of his death in 1874, and was buried in the Lexington Cemetery on June 7, 1874.

STONE, WILLIAM R.

w. 1845-1846—Louisville

William R. Stone was a silver plater working at 609 Main Street in Louisville.

STOY, DAVID C.

w. 1844-1849—Louisville

David C. Stoy was a jeweler and watchmaker. During 1844 and 1845 he was employed as a watch manufacturer at James I. Lemon's store. From 1845 to 1849 the Louisville city directories list him as both a jeweler and a watchmaker at 63 Fourth Street, and boarding at the Taylor House. He was buried in Cave Hill Cemetery in Louisville, but the date of interment is not known.

THOMPSON, JOSEPH S.

w. 1832—Louisville

Joseph S. Thompson, silversmith, appears in Louisville's first city directory which was published in 1832. His business address was Fifth Street between Main and Market.

TODD, WILLIAM

w. 1795—Lexington

d. March 21, 1836.

William Todd was a silversmith, although he evidently followed this trade for only a few years, leaving the art of silversmithing to operate a cotton mill on the south side of Vine Street in Lexington. *The Kentucky Gazette*, on February 10, 1795, carried William Todd's advertisement which read in part "sells watch glasses in the store opposite Love and Brent's Tavern."

TONKREY, SILAS

w. 1812—Shelbyville

Silas Tonkrey, silversmith, worked in Shelby County. A letter from John W. Williamson, of O'Bannon Station, Jefferson County, Kentucky, to Mr. Absalom Matthews, of Shelby County, Kentucky, written December 7, 1872, referred to Silas Tonkrey, silversmith.

VEETER, ANTHONY

w. 1825—Shelbyville

Anthony Veeter was a silversmith who worked in Shelby County. This silversmith was mentioned in a letter from John W. Williamson of O'Bannon Station, Jefferson County, Kentucky, to Mr. Absalom Matthews of Shelby County, Kentucky, written on December 7, 1872.

VIRNEY, ————

w. 1844-1845—Louisville

The Louisville city directory for 1844-45 lists "———— Virney, silversmith" on the east side of Third, between Chestnut and Walnut Streets.

WAIT, EDGAR S.

w. 1848—Louisville

The 1848 Louisville city directory lists Edgar S. Wait, jeweler, at Richard E. Smith's shop. No other record of this man has been found.

WARRINER, S. W.

w. 1845-1846—Louisville

S. W. Warriner was a silversmith who appeared in Louisville briefly. The Louisville city directory for the year 1845-46 carried his advertisement:

"S. W. WARRINER

Manufacturer and Dealer In

JEWELERY AND SILVER WARE,

No. 467 Market, s. side, between 3d and 4th sts,

WATCHES AND JEWLRY neatly repaired."

WERNE, JOSEPH, SR.

    b. May 10, 1808—Germany
    d. March 2, 1858—Louisville
    w. 1832-1858—Louisville

Joseph Werne, Sr., silversmith, was born in Germany on May 10, 1808, and came to Louisville about 1832. The Louisville City Court records show that Joseph Werne, Sr., took out naturalization papers on August 7, 1839. He was a member of the firm of Speigelhalder and Werne from 1836 until his death on March 2, 1858.

He married Charity Susan Krantz, July 1, 1836, in Louisville. Their son, Joseph Werne, Jr., born April 16, 1837, was also a silversmith. He formed a partnership with John Kitts in 1859 which lasted until 1874. He was married to Rosa Melissa Rodney May 29, 1862, and died in Louisville on May 10, 1903.

WEST, EDWARD, JR.

    b. 1757—Virginia
    d. August 23, 1827—Lexington
    w. 1785-1827—Lexington

Edward West, Jr., silversmith, clock- and watchmaker, gunsmith and inventor, was born in Virginia in 1757, the son of Edward and Elizabeth Mills West of Stafford County, Virginia. While still a resident of Virginia, Edward West, Jr., married Sarrah Brown (born 1756, died 1824), the daughter of Samuel and Maria Creed Brown. Twelve children were born to Edward West, Jr., and his wife Sarrah, the most famous of them being William Edward West who was born December 10, 1788, in Lexington. William Edward West was destined to become one of the outstanding portrait painters of his day. His work was exhibited in Paris in 1824 and 1825, at the Royal Academy in London from 1826 to 1833, and other exhibits in London until 1837. He returned to America in 1840, and died in Nashville, Tennessee, on November 2, 1857.

The effects of Edward West, Sr., our subject's father, were sold at "public vendue" in Georgetown on July 23, 1793, and it is interesting to note that the executor's advertisement concerning the sale read in part "together with one in-lot in said Town, whereon is a commodious dwelling house, Smith's shop and garden, ..."

Edward West, Jr., came to Kentucky in 1785. Early Kentucky records tell us that he was a taxpayer and large landowner. Eight land grants to him are listed:

    1/11/1783 — 2100 acres — Fayette County
    4/11/1784 — 200 acres — Lincoln County
    1/4/1787 — 2100 acres — Bourbon County
    11/5/1796 — 415 acres — Lincoln County
    11/5/1795 — 1313 acres — Lincoln County
    9/28/1791 — 200 acres — Nelson County
    8/10/1799 — 200 acres — Warren County
    6/26/1806 — 200 acres — Barren County

During August of 1788 he advertised in the *Kentucky Gazette* as follows:

"EDWARD WEST

Respectfully informs the public that he has opened a shop in the Town of Lexington, on high street and carries on the clock and watch making business in its different branches, all those who shall think proper to oblige him with their custom may depend on being faithfully served, and their business compleated in the best manner and on the shortest notice; he has just received a quantity of excellent watch chrystals."

He was advertising in the *Kentucky Gazette* in 1788. In December of 1790 and the first two months of 1791 he advertised:

"WANTED AN APPRENTICE to the GUN and SILVERSMITH'S business.
       EDWARD WEST, JUN."

The February 10, 1795, *Kentucky Gazette* carried the announcement that "Edward West moves his silversmith's shop to Main Street, opposite Bradford's Printing office." Edward West is listed in Lexington's second city directory, published in 1818, as a "Silversmith and Watch Maker, High Street."

It was in 1793 that Edward West invented a steam engine, which he successfully demonstrated on Town Branch at Lexington that same year before a large group of people assembled to see the exciting trial. Several years later, on August 10, 1801, the *Kentucky Gazette* carried the following announcement:

"Edward West, on Thursday last (August 6th) exhibited to the citizens of this town a specimen of a boat worked by steam, applied to oars. The application is simple and from the opinion of good judges will be of great benefit in navigation of the Mississippi and Ohio Rivers. Mr. West intends to apply for a patent for this discovery."

In 1802 he went to Washington to apply for patents on his inventions. July 6, 1802, he secured patents covering his invention of the steamboat and a gun lock, as well as a nail-cutting and heading machine, the rights to which he had sold for $10,000 prior to securing a patent. Models of Mr. West's steamboat and the nail-cutting and heading machine in the patent office were destroyed when the British burned Washington in 1814.

On December 11, 1799, we find Edward West advertising in the *Kentucky Gazette* that he had "Discovered an effectual cure for the Rheumatic Pains and Cramps, by means of Metallic Rings of a particular composition," and he published testimonials of persons helped by wearing the rings. Mr. West's inventive ability led him to further endeavors, and he is also credited with inventing a wirebound cannon, a pistol, a machine for cutting or pressing molding on gutter pipe, and a hemp-breaking machine. He also worked diligently with John Bradford, the editor of the *Kentucky Gazette*, in an attempt to learn the secret of perpetual motion. It was said of him that "he could make or mend anything."

Edward West lived at his shop from 1785 until 1795. During those years he prospered sufficiently to enable him to build a brick home adjoining the shop. The earliest tax records available list "One frame house and one brick house adjoining." In 1798 he mortgaged his property to Lewis West for five hundred pounds, and in December of the same year conveyed to Elizabeth West a large list of household furniture and livestock for the sum of one hundred pounds.

The *Kentucky Gazette*, on July 8, 1806, reported that several silver watches had been stolen from Edward West's shop the night before.

Mr. West served for many years as a member of the Board of Trustees for the City of Lexington, and the Fayette County Order Book A records the allowance of one pound ten shillings to Mr. West for making the first Fayette County seal.

On February 7, 1824, Edward West's wife, Sarrah, died. Two and one-half years later, on August 23, 1827, Edward West died at the age of seventy. Both were buried in the garden of their home on High Street in Lexington. Their bodies were later removed to the Presbyterian Cemetery in Lexington, because ground, including the graveyard, was sold to John Woolley. In the September 1, 1827, issue of *The Kentucky Reporter* this notice appears:

> "DIED—Last Week, Mr. Edward West, an old and highly respectable citizen."

His estate inventory, which was filed November 27, 1827, in the Fayette County Court, lists many pieces of silver and an impressive list of tools. Appraisers of the estate were David A. Sayre, William Poindexter and Henry H. Vaughn.

WHITE, PETER

w. 1832—Louisville

Peter White was a silversmith who appeared in Louisville's first city directory published in 1832. His shop was on Fifth Street between Main and Market. Peter White, Sr., was carried on the Shelby County Tax List 1792-1795, as the owner of one hundred acres of land on Bullskin Creek.

WILSON, J.

b. 1804

d. 1889—Lexington

w. 1838-1839—Lexington

J. Wilson is carried in the 1838-39 Lexington city directory as a silver plater working at 13 N. Mulberry Street (now Limestone). A James Wilson, whose late residence had been Lexington, was interred in the Lexington Cemetery September 9, 1889, age eighty-five.

WINCHESTER, DANIEL F.

w. 1841—Louisville

The Louisville city directory for 1841 lists Daniel F. Winchester, silversmith, at William and A. Cooper's.

WIRT, JOHN

w. 1818—Lexington

John Wirt was a silversmith working at Main-Cross (now Broadway) in 1818. He also was employed by Asa Blanchard at one time.

WOODRUFF, L. AND E.

w. 1811-1815—Lexington

Apparently the firm of L. and E. Woodruff was operated by Ezra Woodruff. The date of the firm's beginning is not known, but when David Sayre came to Lexington in 1811 he was employed by Ezra Woodruff. The firm advertised in Lexington, on June 13, 1812, as silver platers, silversmiths and brass founders. Court records show that Ezra Woodruff failed in 1815.

WOOLRIDGE, JOHN W.

w. 1819—Frankfort

John W. Woolridge, silversmith, was advertising in the newspapers of Frankfort in 1819.

WRIGHT, JOHN F.

w. 1841-1848—Louisville

John F. Wright was a jeweler and watchmaker. He appeared in the Louisville city directories from 1841 until 1848. In 1841 he was employed as a jeweler at Richard E. Smith's shop. In 1845 he was living above 471 Market Street, and in 1848 his residence is given at 519 Green between Floyd and Preston.

YEISER, FREDERICK

1814-1820—Danville

-1857—Lexington

So far as can be determined, Frederick Yeiser was a jeweler. He was in Danville in 1814, or possibly earlier. The exact date of his move to Lexington is not known, but he was in business there in 1857. The 1859 Lexington city directory lists F. Yeiser and Company, "Watches, Jewelry, Silverware, etc., south east corner Upper and Main."

The marriage of Captain Frederick Yeiser and Miss Lucy Bradford in Danville in December, 1820, was reported in the December 11, 1820, issue of the *Kentucky Gazette*.

YEISER, PHILIP

w. 1814—Danville

w. 1859—Lexington

d. 1859—Lexington

Philip Yeiser, a jeweler, was in Danville in 1814. Some time later he moved to Lexington, and it is possible he was a member of the firm of F. Yeiser and Company which was advertising in Lexington in 1859. He died in 1859 and is interred in the Lexington Cemetery.

YOUNG, THOMAS

w. 1789-1793—Lexington
Danville

Thomas Young was an early silversmith of Lexington and Danville. He appeared on the Fayette County Census in December, 1789. On June 10, 1789, John Coburn and his wife, Mary, of Woodford County, Kentucky, deeded land in Lexington to Thomas Young of Fayette County.

From 1789 to 1793 the *Kentucky Gazette* carried his advertisements, asking all persons indebted to him to "settle their respective balances . . . ." In 1789 Mr. Innis Brent was authorized to transact his business, and in 1791 Mr. Hugh Brentsun was authorized to settle Mr. Young's accounts. Finally, during July, August and September, 1793, Thomas Young advertised in the *Kentucky Gazette* as follows:

> "ALL debts due me, and not discharged before the 15th of August next, will be put into the hands of a proper officer to collect. Any person inclining to pay, will find my books and papers, with mr. H. Brent jun of Lexington."

Apparently he carried on the silversmith's business in Danville after leaving Lexington.

ZUMAR, GEORGE A.

w. 1831-1849—Louisville

George A. Zumar was a jeweler and watchmaker whose name was spelled in many ways in the Louisville city directories, in histories and articles. His name appeared as Zeuma, Zoomer, Zumar, Zeumar, Zuma, Zeumer and Zumer.

The *Louisville Daily Journal* of September 20, 1831, carried Evans C. Beard's announcement of his association with Mr. "George A. Zeumer" under the firm name of E. C. Beard and Company. Their advertisement in the 1832 Louisville city directory shows that the firm sold silverplate, watches, clocks, music, pianofortes, percussion guns, pistol caps and lamps of every description.

As announced in *The Kentucky Reporter* of November 28, 1831, George A. "Zeumer" and Miss Ann P. Satterwhite, daughter of Mann Satterwhite, were married in Fayette County in November of 1831. In 1836 they were living on the east side of Seventh between Main and Market where they remained until 1848 when their address became 203 Green Street, between Seventh and Eighth.

UNCONFIRMED LIST
of
KENTUCKY SILVERSMITHS

Unconfirmed List of Kentucky Silversmiths

The following men have been classed as silversmiths by some sources. While the authors have not been able positively to verify them as silversmiths, they are listed in the hope that additional information may one day establish them definitely among the silversmiths of Kentucky.

ARMER, D. P.

D. P. Armer worked in Richmond, Kentucky; date unknown. His marriage to Anna Farley in 1868, recorded in Madison County, Kentucky, Marriage Book 10, page 86, would indicate he was not working prior to 1850.

BARLOW, EDWARD C.

Served his apprenticeship under Thomas Jefferson Shepard of Georgetown. Born in 1829, he probably was not in business for himself prior to 1850.

BEAUCHAMP, J.

It has been stated that this man worked in Bowling Green 1840-1850.

BEGGS AND SMITH

This firm probably operated in Louisville; date unknown.

BEST, B., AND COMPANY

There is a possibility this firm operated in Louisville, although they do not appear in city directories before 1850.

BRYAN, JAMES

No information has been found to establish when or where this man worked. In 1932 Miss Mabel Weaks of Louisville copied the following information from labels on silver exhibits in the D.A.R. Museum in Washington, D. C.:

"No. 1889. Silver tea spoon – Maker: JAMES BRYAN, Brother of Col. Wm. Bryan, Founder of Bryan's Station. Presented by Mrs. Eugene Howard Ray, Kentucky."

"No. 2210. Small salt spoon. Used by Gov. Isaac Shelby, first Governor of Kentucky. Presented by Mrs. Clarence F. Bryan, Fincastle Chapter, Kentucky."

CASKELL, SAMUEL
This man apparently worked in Louisville; date unknown.

EVANS, W. R.
It has been stated that W. R. Evans was working in Covington, Kentucky, in 1850.

GARNER AND STEWART
Eli C. Garner, Sr., and George W. Stewart are reputed to have been in business together in Lexington at one time. If so, the partnership was probably in existence after 1850.

GREENER, MAX
This man is reputed to have worked in Shelbyville; date unknown.

GREGG, WILLIAM
It has been said this man worked in Lexington from 1813 to 1821.

HARDY, J. H.
A man named ——— Hardy has been placed in Lexington in 1820. There is a possibility it was J. H. Hardy, but it has not been proven they were one and the same.

HEASLEY, SAMUEL
This man has been credited with working in Winchester 1847-1852.

HUMBLE, MICHAEL
No proof has been found that Michael Humble ever worked in silver. He was making pewter spoons and plates in 1779 for the early settlers of Louisville. He was also a gunsmith, with his place of business on Twelfth Street in Louisville. He was a private on the muster roll of Captain Harrod's Company in 1779.

JONES, JOHN W., AND SON
It has been said this firm worked in Mt. Sterling; date unknown.

KINSEY, EDWARD AND DAVID
It has not been definitely established that this firm operated in Kentucky. A ladle in the family of Mrs. Wade Hampton Whitley of Paris is marked "E & D KINSEY," and the date of the ladle has been established as "probably 1835." This would seem to place this firm in Kentucky, since at this time it is known that Edward Kinsey was working in Newport, Kentucky. Mrs. Whitley's grandmother, Mollie Hedges, had spoons marked "E & D KINSEY," bearing the inscription "Prem. B. Co. A. S. 1854." Mollie Hedges was awarded the spoons as premiums for her embroidery entered at the Bourbon County Agricultural Society Fair.

LEDMAN, S. E.
This man is said to have worked in Louisville; date unknown.

LENHART, G.
G. Lenhart is said to have worked in Bowling Green; date unknown.

LINEBAUGH, BEN
This man is said to have been in Russellville in 1825.

McCONNAGHY, ————
It has been said a Mr. McConnaghy worked in Wayne County before 1850; exact date unknown.

McDONALD, CHARLES
This man has been placed in Lexington; date unknown.

McLURE, JAMES
It has been said this man worked in Bowling Green from 1840 to 1881.

McLURE AND FUSSELLI

This partnership is reputed to have been located in Bowling Green; date unknown.

PEACOCK, THOMAS

Thomas Peacock was born in 1818. He is said to have worked in Lancaster from 1845 to 1874; however, no proof of his activities as a silversmith have been discovered. He remained a bachelor until May 9, 1872, when, at the age of 54, he married Margaret Johnson, aged 48. He was obviously a man of some means, for he purchased many pieces of land from 1845 to 1874, which are the earliest and the latest dates in which deeds were recorded to him. His first purchase consisted of two lots in Lancaster, Kentucky, known on the town plat as lots number sixty-eight and ninety-four. His last purchase, on July 28, 1874, was two parcels of land, for which he paid $700 cash and executed a twelve-month note for an additional $700, the note bearing interest at ten per cent.

RUSSELL, ARTHUR

Arthur Russell is said to have worked in Bardstown; date unknown.

RUSSELL, WILLIAM

It has been stated that this man was a silversmith who worked in Nelson County, but no record of him has been discovered by the authors, neither has a date been established.

RUSSELL, WILLIAM, AND SON

This firm has been placed in Bardstown from 1840 to 1860.

SIMPSON, S.

It has been said S. Simpson worked in Hopkinsville; date unknown. A "Solomon" Simpson appears on the Shelby County Tax List of 1797, and he was a taxpayer in Fayette County in 1790. A "Sydonia" Simpson was interred in the Lexington Cemetery, April 30, 1871.

SMITH, HARTLEY T.

Bowling Green has been given as this man's place of business from 1850 to 1860.

SMITH AND BEGGS

Louisville has been named as the city in which this firm was located; date unknown.

TALBOT, W. H.

W. H. Talbot has been termed a silversmith and an inventor of a multiplying reel. Where and when he worked is not known. A W. H. Talbott and Company is listed in the city directories of Indianapolis, Indiana, from 1855 to 1865.

VAN HOY, SHELBY

Shelbyville has been named as this man's place of residence. J. S. Chandler of Campbellsville, Kentucky, wrote the authors at the request of Mrs. Shelby S. Van Hoy, Jr., stating: "I can tell you that Mr. Shelby S. Van Hoy, Jr., moved to Shelbyville from Campbellsville about 1907 and opened a jewelry store and practiced there as an optometrist until his death in 1937. His father was not in business."

SKETCHES OF MARKS USED BY SOME OF THE EARLY KENTUCKY SILVERSMITHS AND JEWELERS

The following sketches of marks found on early Kentucky silver are typical examples of the marks used by Kentucky silversmiths and jewelers to identify their work.

A complete list of the marks used by each of the silversmiths and jewelers discussed in this work is impossible to compile, since examples of the marks used by some of them have not yet been found.

The fact that most of these early artisans used their surname, alone or with their initials, simplifies the identification of their work. Few Kentucky craftsmen identified their silver with initials only.

Sketches of Marks 113

```
JOHN B AKIN
    DANVILLE KY                    JOHN B. AKIN
STANDARD
    PLK


JOHN B AKIN
   DANVILLE
      KY                            JOHN B. AKIN
   PL KRIDER
     PHILA PA


JOHN B AKIN
   DANVILLE
      KY                            JOHN B. AKIN
   PL KRIDER
      STANDARD
```

| T. AYRES | THOMAS R. J. AYRES |

| S-AYRES-LEX.K. | SAMUEL AYRES |

| D P Armer Richmond Ky | D. P. ARMER |

| E C BARLOW | EDWARD C. BARLOW |

JAMES P. BARNES

Mark	Maker
BEARD	EVANS C. BEARD
BLANCHARD	ASA BLANCHARD
A·BLANCHARD	ASA BLANCHARD
A.BLANCHARD	ASA BLANCHARD
A.BLANCHARD	ASA BLANCHARD
BLANCHARD	ASA BLANCHARD
J.DRAPER	JOSEPH DRAPER
W & A COOPER	WILLIAM & ARCHABALD COOPER
W R EVANS	W. R. EVANS
W.R.EVANS PREMIUM	W. R. EVANS
H.FLETCHER	HENRY FLETCHER
FLETCHER & BENNETT	FLETCHER AND BENNETT
E.C.GARNER	ELI C. GARNER
GARNER	ELI C. GARNER

Sketches of Marks   115

Mark	Name
D.C. FULTON	DAVID C. FULTON
LEX KY / GARNER & WINCHESTER	GARNER AND WINCHESTER
GARNER & WINCHESTER	GARNER AND WINCHESTER

10 OZ 15   B.C. PREMIUM A.S.

Mark	Name
HALEY PARIS KY	G. W. OR P. HALEY
W. HARDMAN / LEX KY	WILLIAM HARDMAN
JHickman	JOHN HICKMAN
H. HUDSON / LOUISVILLE	HENRY HUDSON
HUDSON & DOLFINGER / LOUISVILLE	HUDSON AND DOLFINGER
H HYMAN	HENRY W. HYMAN
H HYMAN · RHD	HENRY W. HYMAN
W. KENDRICK / LOUISVILLE	WILLIAM KENDRICK

Sketches of Marks

WM. KENDRICK
LOUISVILLE — WILLIAM KENDRICK

WM. KENDRICK — WILLIAM KENDRICK

[KENDRICK] — WILLIAM KENDRICK

JOHN KITTS — JOHN KITTS

J. KITTS — JOHN KITTS

[J. KITTS] — JOHN KITTS

COIN JOHN KITTS C+R — JOHN KITTS

KITTS & WERNE (H) ◆ (S) ✳ — KITTS AND WERNE

[LEMON + KENDRICK] — LEMON AND KENDRICK

[G Lenhart] — G. LENHART

[W. P. LOOMIS] — WORHAM P. LOOMIS

[B. B. MARSH] [PARIS KY] — BENEDICT BEAL MARSH

[B. B. MARSH] [RICHMOND KY] — BENEDICT BEAL MARSH

[T. K. MARSH] [PARIS KY] — THOMAS KING MARSH

[T. K. MARSH] — THOMAS KING MARSH

Sketches of Marks

Mark	Name
A.G. MEDLEY	ANDREW G. MEDLEY
POINDEXTER	WM. A. OR WM. P. POINDEXTER
W. POINDEXTER	WM. A. OR WM. P. POINDEXTER
B.M. RIGGS	BENJAMIN McKENNY RIGGS
Wm RUSSELL & SON / Sindner / STANDARD	WILLIAM RUSSELL AND SON
W.M. SAVAGE	WILLIAM M. SAVAGE
J.S. SHARRARD	JAMES S. SHARRARD
J.S. SHARRARD	JAMES S. SHARRARD
T.J. SHEPARD	THOMAS JEFFERSON SHEPARD
J. SIMPSON	JONATHAN SIMPSON
R.E. SMITH	RICHARD EWING SMITH
Smith & Grant	SMITH AND GRANT
SMITH & GRANT	SMITH AND GRANT

 GEORGE W. SNYDER, SR.

F. SPIEGELHALDER   FERDINAND SPIEGELHALDER

G.W. STEWART
LEX. KY.   GEORGE W. STEWART

J. WERNE
  LOUISVILLE
      KY   JOSEPH WERNE, SR.
P.L.K. ✚
  STANDARD

BIBLIOGRAPHY

Bibliography

BOOKS, CATALOGUES AND ARTICLES

Allen, William B. *History of Kentucky.* Louisville. 1872.

Allison, Young E. *A Chapter Of Trappist History In Kentucky.* Louisville. 1926.

American Biographical Publishing Company. *Memorial History Of Louisville From Its First Settlement To The Year 1896.* Vol. I and Vol. II.

Ardery, Mrs. William Breckenridge. *Historical Scrapbook, Bourbon County, Kentucky, Celebrating the 150th Anniversary of The Founding of Her County Seat Hopewell (Paris).* Lexington. 1939.

Ardery, Mrs. William Breckenridge. *Kentucky Court And Other Records, Vol. II. From Original Court Entries.* Lexington. 1932.

Ardery, Mrs. William Breckenridge. *Kentucky Records—Early Wills and Marriages.* Daughters of the American Revolution of Kentucky. 1926.

Armstrong, J. M., Company. *The Biographical Encyclopaedia Of Kentucky Of The Dead And Living Men Of The Nineteenth Century.* Cincinnati. 1878.

Barr, Lockwood. "Kentucky Silver And Its Makers." *Antiques.* July, 1945.

Baylor, Orval W. *Early Times In Washington County, Kentucky.* Cynthiana. 1942.

Bogardus, Carl R. *The Early History Of Gallatin County, Kentucky—1798-1949.* Warsaw. 1948.

Bridwell, Margaret M. "Asa Blanchard—Early Kentucky Silversmith." *Antiques.* March, 1940.

Bridwell, Margaret M. "Edward West, Silversmith And Inventor." *The Filson Club History Quarterly,* Vol. 21, No. 4. October, 1947.

Bridwell, Margaret M. "House Of Kendrick." *The Filson Club History Quarterly.* Vol. 22, No. 4. October, 1948.

Bridwell, Margaret M. "Kentucky Silver." *Antiques.* November, 1947.

Bridwell, Margaret M. "Kentucky Silversmiths Before 1850." *The Filson Club History Quarterly,* Vol. XVI. 1942.

Bridwell, Margaret M. "Louisville's Early Silversmiths." *The American Antique Journal.* July, 1947.

Century Company, The. *Century Cyclopedia Of Names.* 1914.

Clift, G. Glenn. Register of Kentucky Historical Society—*Kentucky Marriages And Obituaries 1787-1860.* Vol. 36 Nos. 115, 116, 117; Vol. 37 Nos. 118, 119, 120, 121; Vol. 38 No. 122; Vol. 39 Nos. 126, 127, 128 and 129; Vol. 40 Nos. 130, 131, 132, 133; Vol. 42.

Coleman, J. Winston, Jr. "Kentucky Landmarks." *Antiques.* November, 1947.

Currier, Ernest M. *Marks Of Early American Silversmiths.* Portland. 1938.

Cutten, George Barton. *Silversmiths Of Virginia (Together with Watchmakers and Jewelers) from 1694 to 1850.* Richmond. 1952.

Dallas Morning News, The. "Outdoors With Kenneth Faree, Outdoor Editor." (Not dated)

Dunn, Frank C. "Lexington's Noted Pioneer Silversmith And Inventor Left His Own Memorial Here." *Lexington Herald-Leader.* March 2, 1941.

Ensko, Stephen G. C. *American Silversmiths And Their Marks III.* New York. 1948.

Fackler, Calvin Morgan. *Early Days In Danville.* Louisville. 1941.

Farmers Bank and Capital Trust Company. *A Century Of Progress With Frankfort.* Frankfort. 1949.

Field and Stream. "My Old Kentucky Reel." January, 1953.

Gaines, B. O. *History of Scott County.* Vol. I. Georgetown. 1905.

Hall, Mitchel. *Johnson County, Kentucky, A History of the County, and Genealogy of Its People Up to the Year 1927.* Vol. I and Vol. II. Louisville. 1928.

Harrington, Miss Jessie. *Silversmiths Of Delaware 1700-1850.* National Society of Colonial Dames of America in the State of Delaware. Camden. 1939.

Heinemann, Charles Brunk. *First Census Of Kentucky—1790.* Washington, D.C. 1940.

Johnson, L. F. *History Of The Frankfort Cemetery.* Frankfort. 1921.

Johnson, L. F. *The History Of Franklin County, Kentucky.* Frankfort. 1912.

Jones, E. Alfred. *Old Silver of American Churches.* Privately printed for the National Society of Colonial Dames of America. 1913.

Kendrick, William Carnes. *Reminiscences Of Old Louisville.* Mimeographed. Louisville. No date.

Leach, Mary James. "Kentucky's Early Silversmiths Now Gain Recognition." *Courier-Journal.* Louisville. October 30, 1938.

Leavy, William A. "A Memoir Of Lexington And Its Vicinity." *The Register of Kentucky Historical Society.* July, 1942.

Lewis, Mary Sneed. *Reminiscences Of Frankfort Two Years Ago.* Written about 1886, according to Bayless Hardin, Secretary, Kentucky Historical Society.

McKee-Bond. *A History Of Anderson County 1780-1936.* Begun in 1884 by Major Lewis W. McKee—Concluded in 1936 by Mrs. Lydia K. Bond. Frankfort. 1936.

Newcomb, Rexford. *Architecture In Old Kentucky.* Urbana. 1953.

New York, The Metropolitan Museum of Art *Catalogue Of An Exhibition Of Silver Used In New York, New Jersey And The South.* Part III, p. 13. New York. November 6 to December 31, 1911.

Perkins, H. E. *A Record Of The Family Of Roswell Smith, Son of Steel Smith of Farmington, Connecticut; Windsor, Vermont, and Other Localities With Residents of Descendants so Far as is Known to Date.* 1919.

Perrin, William Henry. *History Of Bourbon, Scott, Harrison And Nicholas Counties.* Chicago. 1882.

Perrin, William Henry. *History Of Fayette County, Kentucky.* Chicago. 1882.

Phillips, Ulrich B. *Life And Labor In The Old South.* Boston. 1937.

Price, General Samuel Woodson. *The Old Masters Of The Bluegrass; Jouett, Bush, Grimes, Frazer, Morgan, Hart.* Louisville. 1902.

Ranck, George W. *History of Lexington, Kentucky—Its Early Annals and Recent Progress.* Cincinnati. 1872.

Scribner's Sons, Charles. *Dictionary Of American Biography.* 1928-1936.

Staples, Charles R. *The History Of Pioneer Lexington, Kentucky 1779-1806.* Lexington. 1939.

Thorn, C. Jordan. *Handbook Of American Silver And Pewter Marks.* New York. 1949.

Webster's Biographical Dictionary. 1943.

White, James T., and Company. *National Cyclopaedia Of American Biography.* 1893-1921.

Willis, George L., Sr. *History Of Shelby County, Kentucky.* Louisville. 1929.

DIRECTORIES

Louisville—First City Directory —1832
          City Directory   —1836
          Ibid.   —1838-39
          Ibid.   —1841
          Ibid.   —1843-44
          Ibid.   —1844-45
          Ibid.   —1845-46
          Ibid.   —1848
          Ibid.   —1848-49
          Ibid.   —1851-52
          City Directories   —1852-1875

Lexington—First Printed City Directory—1806
          City Directory   —1818
          Lexington City Directory
            and Fayette County   —1838-39
          Lexington City Directory   —1859
          Ibid.   —1864-65

VARIOUS RECORDS

Kentucky State Historical Society Records

Lexington Cemetery Records

Cave Hill Cemetery, Louisville, Records

The Filson Club Records

NEWSPAPERS

The Kentuckian-Citizen (A Voice of The Bluegrass Since 1807). Paris, Kentucky.

The Kentucky Gazette. Lexington. September 1, 1787; May 17, 1788, August 9, 1788, August 16, 1788, August 23, 1788, November 29, 1788, December 6, 1788, December 13, 1788, December 20, 1788, December 27, 1788; January 3, 1789, January 10, 1789, January 17, 1789, January 24, 1789, May 11, 1789, June 6, 1789, June 13, 1789, June 20, 1789, June 27, 1789, July 4, 1789, July 11, 1789, July 18, 1789, July 25, 1789, August 1, 1789, August 8, 1789, August 15, 1789, August 22, 1789, August 29, 1789, September 5, 1789, September 12, 1789, September 19, 1789, September 26, 1789, December 12, 1789; January 2, 1790, January 13, 1790, January 23, 1790, January 30, 1790, February 6, 1790, February 13, 1790, February 20, 1790, Febuary 27, 1790, March 6, 1790, March 15, 1790, May 31, 1790, June 22, 1790, July 12, 1790, July 19, 1790, December 4, 1790, December 11, 1790, December 18, 1790; January 1, 1791, January 8, 1791, January 15, 1791, January 22, 1791, January 29, 1791, February 5, 1791, February 12, 1791, February 19, 1791, June 4, 1791, June 18, 1791, June 25, 1791, July 2, 1791, July 9, 1791, July 16, 1791, October 8, 1791, October 29, 1791, November 5, 1791, November 12, 1791,

November 19, 1791, November 26, 1791, December 3, 1791, December 10, 1791, December 17, 1791, December 24, 1791, December 31, 1791; January 7, 1792, January 14, 1792, January 21, 1792, January 28, 1792, February 4, 1792, February 11, 1792, February 18, 1792, February 25, 1792, March 3, 1792, March 10, 1792, March 17, 1792, June 9, 1792, June 23, 1792, July 7, 1792, July 14, 1792, July 21, 1792, July 28, 1792, August 4, 1792, August 11, 1792, August 18, 1792, August 25, 1792, September 1, 1792, September 8, 1792, November 24, 1792, December 1, 1792, December 8, 1792, December 15, 1792, December 22, 1792, December 29, 1792; January 5, 1793, January 12, 1793, January 19, 1793, January 26, 1793, February 2, 1793, February 9, 1793, February 16, 1793, February 23, 1793, March 2, 1793, March 16, 1793, March 23, 1793, March 30, 1793, April 6, 1793, April 13, 1793, April 20, 1793, April 27, 1793, May 11, 1793, May 18, 1793, June 1, 1793, June 8, 1793, June 15, 1793, June 22, 1793, June 29, 1793, July 6, 1793, July 13, 1793, July 27, 1793, August 3, 1793, August 10, 1793, August 17, 1793, August 24, 1793, August 31, 1793, September 7, 1793; February 22, 1794, April 12, 1794, April 19, 1794, April 26, 1794, May 3, 1794; February 10, 1795; January 21, 1799, December 11, 1799; August 10, 1801; May 14, 1802; July 12, 1803; December 20, 1804; August 24, 1805; September 18, 1806, November 17, 1806; November 13, 1810; June 4, 1811; April 29, 1816; January 6, 1817; August 28, 1818; April 21, 1819; December 11, 1820; September 20, 1838.

The Western Citizen. Paris, Kentucky. September 1, 1813; November 25, 1817; 1831.

The Observer And Reporter. Lexington. May 27, 1835; January 1, 1840; February 21, 1846, April 4, 1846; January 2, 1847.

Kentucky Reporter. Lexington. June 21, 1820; November 24, 1823; September 20, 1824, October 7, 1824, November 29, 1824; August 18, 1825; September 1, 1827; May 4, 1831, November 28, 1831.

Kentucky Observer And Reporter. Lexington. July 1, 1835; March 21, 1836, May 30, 1836, October 12, 1836, November 16, 1836; September 19, 1838; May 23, 1846; September 22, 1847; November 25, 1848.

Lexington Morning Herald. Lexington. October 23, 1899, October 27, 1899; April 26, 1902; January 30, 1903.

Lexington Herald-Leader. Lexington. May 12, 1940; February 9, 1941, March 2, 1941.

Western World. Frankfort. July 19, 1806, August 9, 1806, August 16, 1806, November 1, 1806; January 15, 1807, March 26, 1807, November 12, 1807.

Daily Yeoman. Frankfort. January 2, 1846; December 20, 1865; December 3, 1881.

Weekly Yeoman. Frankfort. January 2, 1877.

The Tri-Weekly Kentucky Yeoman. Frankfort. March 4, 1851; December 19, 1874; December 30, 1875; December 21, 1876; December 13, 1877; September 28, 1882, November 21, 1882. Checked to No. 12, Vol. I.

The Commonwealth. Frankfort. June 25, 1833 and prior. April 10, 1839; July 13, 1841; February 11, 1842; February 3, 1843, June 20, 1843; November 11, 1846; January 29, 1850; April 27, 1852, August 31, 1852, December 28, 1852; May 16, 1854; January 1, 1856; December 22, 1865; April 27, 1866; December 12, 1878.

Argus Of Western America. Frankfort. Checked to July 12, 1826. No. 21, Vol. XIX.

The Standard. Bardstown. October 25, 1906.

The Frankfort Commonwealth. Frankfort. November 15, 1834; January 28, 1835; October 8, 1869.

Daily Commonwealth. Frankfort. January 1, 1844, June 8, 1844.
Semi-Weekly Commonwealth. Frankfort. July 27, 1866.
Tri-Weekly Commonwealth. Frankfort. July 19, 1852; May 1, 1854; May 31, 1854.
The Dallas Morning News. (Clipping undated)
The Louisville Daily Journal. Louisville. November 24, 1830; September 20, 1831, November 10, 1831; August 15, 1839; July 11, 1850.
The Farmers Library and Ohio Intelligencer. February 3, 1803, March 10, 1803.
The Western Courier. (From the private complete collection of Miss Mary Verhoeff, Vice-President, The Filson Club, Louisville, and used with her permission.) March 20, 1816, April 10, 1816, May 9, 1816.
Louisville Daily Focus. Louisville. November 2, 1831.
The Louisville Times. Louisville. July 23, 1929.
Courier-Journal. Louisville. October 7, 1829; October 30, 1938.
Delaware Journal. February 3, 1832.
Maysville Eagle. Maysville. December 24, 1816.
Herald-Post. Louisville. October 7, 1928.

STATE AND COUNTY RECORDS

Virginia Legislature Records regarding establishment of Kentucky County, 1776.
Virginia Legislature Records regarding establishment of Frankfort, 1786.
Virginia Legislature Records regarding charter granted, authorizing the establishment of the town of Hopewell (Paris) in 1789.
Stafford County, Virginia, Birth and Marriage Records.
Kentucky Legislature, Acts of 1834, Chapter 554, p. 787, establishing the town of Paintsville, Floyd County.
Kentucky Legislature Records regarding procuring suitable gold medals in 1860 for surviving officers and soldiers of the Kentucky Volunteers participating in the engagement between the Americans and the British on Lake Erie, September 10, 1813.
Kentucky Legislature—First Session commenced June 4, 1792.
Kentucky Constitutions—Danville, April 19, 1792
                              Frankfort, August 17, 1799
                              Frankfort, June 11, 1850
                              Frankfort, September 28, 1891
Kentucky Legislature—Act of 1806, establishing the "Old Bank of Kentucky."
First Census of Kentucky—1790. Prepared under the supervision of Charles Brunk Heinemann, Washington, D.C. Copyrighted 1940 by Charles Brunk Heinemann.
                              Fayette County—1789
                              Fayette County—1790
                              Madison County—1789
                              Lincoln County—1790
                              Nelson County—1792
Barren County Marriage Records. Ibid. Will Book 3, p. 327.
Bourbon County—Deposition filed by William Steele (501). Ibid. Complete Records and suits. Ibid. Entries, Book 14, p. 133. Ibid. Random Notes from Suits filed in office of Circuit Clerk.

Christian County Will Record.

Fayette County Entries, Book 1, pps. 270 and 418; Book 2, p. 36; Book 3, p. 426; Book 4, p. 6; Ibid. Court Records; ibid. Circuit Court Deed Book A; ibid. Will Abstracts; ibid. Will Book B, p. 24; ibid. Order Book A, p. 19.

Floyd County Tax List, October 4, 1837; ibid. Entries, Books 1 and 2, pp. 91, 92.

Garrard County Marriage Bond Book 11, p. A.

Harrison County Order Book A.

Jefferson County Will Book 4, p. 281.

Johnson County Order Book 53, p. 195; ibid. Act establishing town of Paintsville in 1834—Chap. 554, p. 787, Acts 1834. Sec. 7.

Madison County Will Book G, p. 280; ibid. Marriage, Book 10, p. 86.

Mason County Will Book F, p. 283; ibid. Will Book G, p. 219; ibid. Will Book P, p. 77; ibid. Deed Book R, p. 443; ibid. Deed Book 35, p. 303; ibid. Deed Book 60, p. 312; ibid. Deed Book Y, p. 60; ibid. Court Order Book K, p. 234; ibid. Court Order Book L, p. 107.

Nelson County Will Record, Book 4, p. 557; ibid. Will Record, Book 12, pp. 453, 455, 456; ibid. Order Book of 1817.

Scott County, Kentucky, Burnt Records, Deed Book 1, p. 24.

Shelby County First Tax List 1792-1795; ibid. Tax List 1796; ibid. Tax List 1797; ibid. Record of October 12, 1917; ibid. Marriages 1794; ibid. Marriages 1792-1800.

Simpson County Will Book 1, p. 147, Clerk's office.

Woodford County Will Book A.

MISCELLANEOUS RECORDS

Two Suits—Withers vs. Miller. (Re: Second company to improve on Hinkson's fork of Licking in 1775.)

The Kentucky Agricultural and Mechanical Association, incorporated December 7, 1850, dissolved spring of 1872.

The Kentucky Agricultural and Mechanical Society, organized spring of 1872.

Meeting of Mexican War Veterans in Frankfort, February, 1880.

Danville and Houstonville Turnpike Road (usually called the Lexington Turnpike) incorporated 1844.

Frankfort City Records (Re: Consolidation of North Frankfort and South Frankfort in 1850, and settlement of property rights, Act of 1880.)

Lexington City Records (Re: Incorporation of Lexington.)

Louisville City Records—February 13, 1828 Act of Incorporation passed, making Louisville a city.

Genealogy of the Barlow family.

Diary kept by Edward Callistus Barlow 1856-1896, owned by Dr. Edward Callistus Barlow of Georgetown, Kentucky.

Bible Records—Adair Bible in the possession of Mrs. John Towles, Paris, Kentucky. Family Bible in the possession of Aria Harrison Newman (Mrs. Charles William), Indianapolis, Indiana.

INDEX

Index

Names of Kentucky Craftsmen 1785-1850 in italics

Adair, R. F., 1
Adams, C. J., 1
Akin, John B., vii, 1, 53, 113
Akin, William, 1, 2
Akin, William Edwin, 1
Allen, Captain David, 10
Allison, Mr. and Mrs. Richard,
Alrich, Jacob N., 2
Alrich, J. N., and S. W. Warriner, 2
Amiss, Miss Ann, 2
Amos, Cornelius, 2, 12
Anderson, Andrew, 2, 3, 14
Ardery, Julia S. (Mrs. W. M. Breckenridge),
Armer, D. P., 105, 113
Arnold, James G., 7
Arnold, Margaret, 7
Atkinson, William O., 3, 45
Austin, Stephen, 37
Ayres and Beard, 4
Ayres, Dorothy, 5
Ayres, Ebenezer Byram, 3
Ayres, Elias, 3, 4, 10, 11
Ayres, E., and Company, 4
Ayres and Hiter, 6
Ayres, Samuel, vii, 4, 5, 6, 45, 113
Ayres, Dr. Samuel, 6, 66, 69
Ayres, Silas, 3
Ayres, Thomas R. J., 5, 6, 66, 80, 113

Bacon College, 38
Baird, Mary, 7
Baird, Pleasant H., 7, 40, 71
Baird, Pleasant H., Jr., 7
Bank of Danville, 1
Bank of Kentucky (Maysville), 48
Baptist [Pioneer] Cemetery, 31
Barlow, Bettie, 8
Barlow, Edward C., xiv, 105, 113
Barlow, Miss Elizabeth, 8
Barlow, Miss Frankie, 82, 83
Barlow, Henry, 8
Barlow, James Madison, 7, 8
Barlow, Mary, 8
Barlow, Milt G., 8
Barlow, Thomas, 8
Barlow, William, 8
Barnes, James P., vii, 8, 9, 52, 113
Barrett, Robert, 10
Beal, John J., 10
Beal, Patsy (Steele), 91
Beal, Theodore L., 10
Beard and Ayres, 11, 83
Beard, Evans C., 3, 4, 10, 11, 51, 102, 114
Beard, E. C., and Company, 2, 11, 12, 51, 102

Beasley, William, 59
Beatty, Elizabeth, 82
Beauchamp, J., 105
Beggs, William, 12, 39, 65
Beggs and Smith, 105
Bennett, Charles Fletcher, 12, 30, 31
Bennett and Fletcher, 12
Bennett, Fletcher and Co., 12, 31
Bergantz and Frentz, 13
Bergantz, Peter W., 13
Best, B., and Co., 105
Best, John, 13
Blackburn, ———, 13
Blanchard, Asa, vii, ix, x, 2, 3, 13, 14, 15, 16, 17, 27, 34, 38, 42, 55, 100, 114
Blanchard, Horace F., 17
Blanchard, Mary L., 17
Blanchard, Rebecca, 16, 17
Bogaert, Victor, Jr., xiv, 34
Bogaert, Victor, Jewelry Co., XI, 34, 93
Boone, George, 59
Bordersen, Christian, 17
Boss, Mrs. Lula Reed, xiv,
Bourbon County Agricultural Society Fair, 107
Bourbon County Anglers Association, 88, 89
Bradford, Fielding, 14
Bradford, John, 99
Bradford, Miss Lucy, 101
Bradford's Printing Office, 98
Bradford, Simon, 14, 17
Branch Bank of Louisville (Paducah), 87
Brannin, Daniel, 87
Bransford, Mary, 29
Brent, H., Jr., 102
Brent, Innis, 102
Brentsun, Hugh, 102
Brigham, Thomas, 17
Brookway and Bacon, 17
Brown, Maria Creed, 97
Brown, Samuel, 97
Brown, Sarrah, 97
Brown, William, 45
Bryan, Mrs. Clarence F., 105
Bryan, James, 105
Bryan, Colonel William, 105
Bryan's Station, 105
Bryant, Butler, 18, 23
Bryson, Edmund A., 18
Bryson, Edward A., 18, 31
Burke, Edmund K., 18, 39
Burnett, B. L., 18
Bush, Catherine Slough, 18
Bush, Philip, 18, 19

Bush, Philip, Jr., 18, 19
Byram, Mary, 3
Byrne, John, 19

Cachot, Felix Ferjeux, 19, 20, 21, 36, 37
Calvary Church (Louisville), 52
Calvert, Thomas G., 94
Carpenter, Ann, 41
Cashot, Felix F., ix, 20, 21
Caskell, Samuel, 106
Caswell, Samuel, 21, 39
Cave Hill Cemetery, xiv, 12, 21, 28, 30, 36, 39, 45, 52, 54, 64, 71, 95
Centre College (Danville), 49
Chambers, Captain, 69
Chandler, J. S., xiv, 109
Chapel, H., 21
Choate, Stephen D., 21
Christian Baptist Female College, 38
Christian, Berg, 13
Christy, Thomas, 22
Clark, E., Jr., 44
Clark, General George Rogers, 38
Clay, General Green, 16
Clay, Henry, 16, 33, 60, 63
Clay, Samuel, 62
Coburn, John, 102
Coburn, Mary, 102
Coleman, Catharine E., 33
Coleman, Covington, 46
Coleman, David S., 15
Coleman, Eliza, 48
Coleman, Francis, 46
Coleman, J. Winston, Jr., 15, 35

Coleman, Polly, 46
Conery, A., 22, 58, 59
Connelly, Susan J., 25
Cooper, Allefer, 44
Cooper, Archabald, 22, 23
Cooper, Leven, 44
Cooper, William, 23
Cooper, William and Archabald, ii, vii 18, 22, 23, 34, 100, 114
Corbin, Joshua, 60
Cornwallis, Lord, 8
Cown, Polly, 41
Crab, Jared, 24
Craig, Margaret, 29
Craig, William, 29
Crookshanks, A., 7
Crutcher, Henry, Jr., 59
Crutcher, Laura Boone, 59
Crutcher, Nancy Grubbs, 58, 59
Crutcher, Thomas Graves, 58, 59
Cunningham, Robert, 24
Curtis, D., 24, 39

Daniel, H., 8
Danville Academy Fund, 1
Danville and Houstonville Turnpike Road, 3
Daumon, E. J., and Company, 24
Daumont, Edmund J., 56

Daumont, Peter, 24, 86
Demaree, Mr., xiv
Deposit Bank (Frankfort), 70
DeYoung, Elias, and Co., 24, 25
Dickson, Henry, 25
Ditto, Miss Lucy A., xiv,
Dolfinger, Friederich, 45
Dolfinger, Jacob, 25, 26, 45
Dorsey, Henry C., 26
Downing and Baldwin, 51
Draper, Joseph, 26, 114
Drysdale, William, 52
Dudley, Dr. Benjamin W., 37
Dumesnill, Anthony, 26
Dumont, Alfred A., 52
Dumont, P., 26
Duncan, William, 27
Duncan, William Henry, 27

Easley, George, 16, 27, 34
Eaves, W., and A. Falize, 27
Egerton, Matthew, Jr., 14
Elder, Edward, 27
Episcopal Church (Lexington), 78
Erb, Anna Maria (Driesback), 39
Erb, Elizabeth, 39
Erb, Lawrence, 39
Erens, John, 27
Erwin, Thomas M., 28
Esterle, Jacob R., 28
Ethridge, John E., 28
Eubank, James, 28, 29, 76
Eubank, James and Joseph, 29
Eubank and Jeffries, 28, 76
Eubank, Joseph, 28, 29
Eubank, Rebecca, 49
Evans, W. R., 106, 114
Ewing, Warren B., 29, 81
Ewing, William Kendrick, xiv,

Farley, Anna, 105
Farmer, Joyce, 25
Farmer's Bank (Frankfort), 19
Federal Cavalry Company, 82
Fellows, Cargill and Co., 51
Fellows, Wadsworth and Co., 51
Fielding, Nancy, 50
Filson Club, The, xiii, 16, 74
First Baptist Church of Danville, Mercer County, 5
Flaig, Edward, 30
Flaig, Mrs. Edward, 30
Fletcher and Bennett, 12, 31, 114
Fletcher, Henry, 12, 30, 31, 54, 114
Flournoy, Charles J., 93
Forsythe, George H., 18, 31
Foster, Jeremiah, 31
Frankfort Cemetery, 69, 70
Frankfort Presbyterian Church, 16
Frazer, Alexander, ix, 31, 32, 33, 72
Frazer, Eliza Coleman, 33
Frazer, James, 7, 32

Index   131

Frazer, Nancy, 32
Frazer, Oliver, x, 32
Frazer, Robert, ix, 31, 32, 33, 72
Frazer, Robert, Jr., 16, 33
Frazer, Robert P., 33
Fulton, David C., 33, 70, 115
Fulton, James, 34, 65
Fulton, James C., 23

Galt, Matthew, 72
Gano, Dr. S. F., 82
Garner, Eli, 34, 36
Garner, Eli C., 16, 27, 34, 106, 114
Garner, George, 34
Garner and Stewart, 106
Garner and Winchester, vii, 16, 35, 36, 115
Garnsey, David, 36
Garvan, Mabel Brady, Collection, 64
Gates, Peter M., 20, 21, 36
Gatewood, Charles S., 17
Gayle, George W., 59
Genealogy Room, Indiana State Library, xiii,
Gillaspie, John, 36
Gillespie, Samuel, 36
Gilliatt, Katherine Wakefield (Mrs. C. E.), xiii, xiv, 1, 53, 58, 59
Givens, Ann, 29
Givens, Elizabeth, 29
Givens, George, 29
Givens, Isabella, 29
Givens, James, 29
Givens, Jane, 29
Givens, John, 29
Givens, Patsy, 29
Givens, Samuel, 29
Goetes, Peter, 20, 36, 37
Goldsborough, Mrs. Brice M., xiv,
Graham, Dr. Christopher Columbus, 37, 38
Graham, John, 38
Graham, Robert, 38
Graham Springs, Harrodsburg, 38
Grant, Mr., 86
Grant, William, 14, 38
Graves, George Coe, 14
Graves, Thomas, 59
Gray, Thomas, 39
Greener, Max, 106
Gregg, William, 106
Griffin, George, 12, 18, 21, 39, 50, 65
Griffith, John, 71
Griswold, Francis A., 30
Grubbs, Captain Higgason, 59
Gulick, Elizabeth, 39
Gulick, Nathan, 39, 40
Gulick, Samuel, 7, 39, 40

Haikes, Holme, 40
Hair, Joshua J., 40
Hakes, Holme, 40
Haley, G. W., 40, 115
Haley and Haley, 40
Haley, P., 40, 115

Hall, John, 41
Hall, Robert C., 62
Hallack, Alonzo Corwin, 41
Hallack, Annie, 41
Hallack, Benjamin, 41
Hallack, Polly, 41
Hallack, Thomas, 41
Hammond, Miss Abby V., 78
Hancock, Captain John, 59
Hansbrough, Hamlet, 42
Hardin, Bayless, xiii,
Harding, Newell, x,
Hardman, Jacob N., 42, 45
Hardman, William, 42, 115
Hardy, J. H., 106
Harkness, R. H., 8
Harris, Mr., 51, 86
Harris, Alfred, 42
Harris, Mrs. Hester, 17
Harris, John C., 42, 43, 55, 56
Harris and Kendrick, 43
Harris and Lemon, 51
Harrod's Company, Captain, 106
Hart, Captain Nathaniel G., 27, 50
Hassan, Moses, 43
Hayes, Virginia, xiii,
Hays, Catharine, 86
Headington, William, 43
Healey, George P. R., 33
Heasley, Samuel, 106
Hedges, Mollie, 107
Hensley, Samuel, 44, 91
Herbst, George, 7
Hessen, Moses, 43
Hiatt, Mr. and Mrs. Noble W., vii, 65, 109
Hickman, Captain, 44
Hickman, John, 44, 115
Hinton, William M., 44, 45, 60, 63
Hirschbuhl and Dolfinger, 26
Hiter, John G., 5, 6, 45
Hixson, Rachel Runyon, 40
Hockersmith, S., 21
Hopkins, General, 10
Horton, H. V., 45
Hottenroth, Ignatius, 20, 36, 37
Houston, Mr., 92
Howard, Thomas, 20
Hubbard, A., 20
Hudson and Dolfinger, vii, 53, 115
Hudson, Henry, XI, 3, 25, 26, 42, 45, 53, 70, 71, 115
Hughes, Mr., 87
Humble, Michael, 106
Humphreys, David, 46
Humphreys, Joshua, XV, 46
Huston, Sarah, 49
Hyman, Henry W., 46, 115

Illig, G. P. H., 47
Indiana State Library, xiii,
Indianapolis Public Library, xiii,

Index

Irion, Matt, 47, 54
Irwin, Mason T., 47
Isbell, James, 8
Isbell, Susan, 8
Iturbide, Emperor, 37
Izabell, John, 47

Jacoby, Susannah, 41
Jameson, John D., 48
Jameson, Robert Coleman, 48
January, Andrew McConnell, 48, 49
January, Ephraim, 48
January and Nutman, 49
January-Wood Company, 48
Jeffries, James, 49
Jeffries, Smith, 49, 91
Johnson, Margaret, 108
Johnson, Samuel (or Simeon) W., 49
Johnston, James, 39, 50
Jones, Mr., 51
Jones, John W., and Son, 107
Jones, Mary M., 84
Jones, Mr. and Mrs. W. B., xiv,
Jouett, Matthew H., x, 16

Kaye, Miss Mary, 79
Keeve, G. H., 50
Kendrick, George P., 52
Kendrick, Walter, 50, 51
Kendrick, William, ix, 8, 10, 12, 43, 47, 50, 51, 52, 54, 55, 56, 79, 115, 116
Kendrick, William Carnes, 47, 52
Kendrick, Wm., Jewelers, Inc., vii, xiv, 37
Kendrick, Wm., and Son, 52
Kendrick's, Wm., Sons, 52
Kendrick, William Penton, xiv, 50
Kentucky Agricultural and Mechanical Association, 78
Kentucky Historical Society, xiii,
Kentucky Room, Louisville Public Library. XIX
Kentucky Mounted Volunteers, 69
Kentucky School for the Blind, 52
Kentucky Volunteers, 66
Keyt, William H., 84, 85
Kinsey, David, 54
Kinsey, Edward, 54, 107
Kinsey, Edward and David, 107
Kirkland, Rankin, xiv,
Kitts, John, XI, 53, 54, 58, 79, 86, 97, 116
Kitts, John, and Company, 54
Kitts and Stoy, 54
Kitts and Werne, 54, 116
Klink, John J., 30, 54
Kluth, B. T., 47, 54
Knox, Henry, 55
Krantz, Charity Susan, 97
Krider, Peter L., xv, 1

Lafayette, General, 8, 55
Lafayette College, Easton, Pennsylvania, 40
Lamme, Samuel, 29
Lea, Francis, 55

Ledman, S. E., 107
Leland, Edwin G., 85
Lemon, Mrs. Brainard, xiv,
Lemon, Captain James, 56
Lemon, James Innes, ix, 14, 43, 51, 52, 55, 56, 95
Lemon, James I., and Co., 56
Lemon, James I., and Son, 56
Lemon, James K., 56
Lemon and Kendrick, vii, 51, 54, 55, 56, 57, 116
Lenhart, G., 107, 116
Lexington Branch of the U. S. Bank, 48
Lexington Cemetery, xiii, 34, 44, 74, 95, 100, 101, 108
Lexington Light Infantry, 27, 50
Lexington Public Library, xiii, 6
Lincoln, Abraham, 15
Linebaugh, Ben, 107
Little Black Peter, 20, 21
Loomis and Ralph, 59
Loomis, Worham P., 22, 58, 59, 116
Louisville and Frankfort Railroad, 87
Louisville Public Library, xiii,
Love, James, 59
Luckett, Mr. and Mrs. John W., vii, xiv, 9

Mahin, Thomas S., 59
Marsh, Abram C., 60
Marsh, Beal, 60, 63
Marsh, Beal Crafton, 60
Marsh, Benedict, 60
Marsh, Benedict Beal, vii, ix, 41, 44, 45, 60, 61, 62, 63, 116
Marsh, Dryden, 60
Marsh, Eleanor Corbin, 60, 63
Marsh, Eleanor Russell, 60
Marsh, James Nicholas, 60
Marsh, Miss Jane, vii, xiv, 44, 61, 62, 63
Marsh, Nicholas C., 60
Marsh, Pembrooke, 60
Marsh, Rachel, 60
Marsh, Theodore, 60
Marsh, Thomas King, vii, ix, 41, 45, 60, 61, 62, 63, 116
Marsh, Thomas King, 60
Marshall, John C., 64
Martin's Station, 92
Matthew, Elder, 16
Matthews, Absalom, 80, 96
Matthews, L., 41
Maysville Branch of the Bank of Kentucky, 48
Maysville and Lexington Railroad Company, Northern Division, 48
Maysville Public Library, 7, 40
McCall, Miss Mary, 7
McCarty, Joseph, 71
McCaulley, John A., 64
McConnaghy, ——, 107
McConnel, Andrew, 48
McConnel, Sarah, 48
McConothy, Milton, 40, 51, 64, 86

Index 133

McDannold, ——, 64
McDonald, Charles, 107
McDowell, Dr. Ephraim, 6
McGehee, Benjamin H., 58
McGhee, Dr. L. A., 7
McGrew and Beggs, 65
*McLure and Fussell*i, 108
McLure, James, 107
McMillin, Elizabeth, 29
McMullen, Mrs. Elizabeth, 50
McMurray, Thomas, 65
Mead, Daniel, 34, 65
Medley, Andrew G., 65, 117
Meek, Benjamin F., 66, 67, 68, 69, 89
Meek, J. B., and Company, 66
Meek, Jonathan Fleming, 66, 67, 68, 69, 89
Meek, J. F. and B. F., 68, 69
Meek, J. F., and Company, 68
Meek, J. F., B. F. Meek and B. C. Milam, 69
Meek and Milam, 66, 69
Messick, William, 80
Methodist Church (Louisville), 52
Metropolitan Museum of Art, 14, 16
Milam, Benjamin Cave, 66, 68, 69, 70, 89
Milam, B. C., and Son, 69, 70
Milam, John W., 69, 70
Milam, William, 37
Miles, Mrs. Robert Whitfield, xiv,
Miller, John, 92
Milton, John L., xiv,
Mitchell, Martha, 60
Modeman, George, 86
Morford, Eliza (Mrs. Woodruff), 83
Muer, Mollie, 8
Muir, Mr. and Mrs. John W., xiv,
Murray, William, 70

Newman, Aria Harrison (Mrs. Charles William), xiv, 41
Noel, Beverly, 33, 70
Noel, Washington, 70

O'Bannon Station, 80, 96
Offutt, Eleanor Hume, xiv,
Oliver, Miss Nancy, 32
Ormsby House, 12
Orr, Thomas, 45, 70
Outten, Ephriam, 71
Outten, George F., 71
Outten, Isaac, 71
Outten, Jacob, 71
Outten, Joshua, 71
Outten, Margaret, 71
Outten, Mary, 71
Outten, Milky Jones, 71
Outten, Susan, 71
Outten, William, 71
Owens, Colonel Abram, 87
Owens, Harriet, 87

Pack, Mrs. John, xiv, 1, 42, 63
Park, John, 45, 71

Peacock, Thomas, 108
Pentecost, S., 71
Phillipe, Louis, 33
Phillips and Frazer, 72
Phillips, Thomas, 31, 32, 72, 92
Phillips, William B., 71
Poindexter, C. H., 73
Poindexter, C. H. and W. A., 73
Poindexter, Sarah Higbee, 74
Poindexter, William A., 73, 99, 117
Poindexter, William P., 73, 74, 117
Poindexter, W., and Son, 73, 74
Polk, Dr. Jefferson, 6
Presbyterian Cemetery (Lexington), 99
Presbyterian Church (Danville), 49
Presbyterian Church (Lexington), 78
Presbyterian Church (Maysville), 49
Presbyterian Church (Paris), 72
Presbyterian Female College, 38
Price, General Samuel Woodson, 33

Ralph, Mr., 58
Rampp, John, 74
Rampp, William, 74
Rankin, Adam, 87
Ray, Mrs. Eugene Howard, 105
Reed, Strothers, 7
Reeves, Abner, 30
Reilly, J. C., and Company, 74, 75
Reynolds, Elizabeth Ann, 89
Richardson, George, 75, 91
Riggs, Benjamin McKenny, 40, 75, 76, 117
Riggs, David H., 76
Roberts, James S. H., 76
Roberts, P. D., 76
Robinson, William, 94
Rockcastle Springs, 38
Rodman, General John, 68
Rodney, Rosa Melissa, 97
Royal Academy, London, 97
Russell, Arthur, 108
Russell, William, 108
Russell, William, and Son, 108, 117

Satterwhite, Miss Ann P., 102
Satterwhite, Mann, 102
Savage and Eubank, 76
Savage, William M., 28, 29, 76, 117
Sayre, Abby, 78
Sayre, David A., vii, x, 77, 78, 99, 100
Sayre, Ephraim, 78
Sayre Female Institute, vii, xiv, 77, 78
Sayre, L., 78
Schwing, Johann G., 78
Schwing, John G., 51, 78, 79
Schwing, Maria, 51, 52, 79
Scott, Mr., 54
Scott and Kitts, 79
Scott, T. M., 79
Scott, William D., 79, 80, 86
Scott, W. D., and Company, 80
Scotthorn, ——, 80

Index

Searny, Captain, 87
Sharp, George, 80
Sharrard and Ewing, 81
Sharrard, James S., 29, 81, 82, 117
Sharrard, Judson, 81
Sharrard, William M., 81, 82
Shelby, Isaac, 16, 105
Shepard, Alpheus Xavier Francis, 82, 83
Shepard, Frankie, 82, 83
Shepard, James Madison, 82
Shepard, Samuel, 82, 83
Shepard, Thomas Jefferson, 4, 11, 82, 83, 105, 117
Shepherd, Ephraim, 83
Shockley, Martha Jane, 70
Silliman, Mary Ann, 3
Simpkins, James, 83
Simpson, James, 84
Simpson, Jonathan, ix, 83, 84, 85, 117
Simpson, John Desha, 84
Simpson, S., 108
Simpson, Solomon, 108
Simpson, Sydonia, 108
Simrall, John W. G., 84
Smart, George, 85
Smith, Miss Amanda, 83
Smith and Beggs, 109
Smith, George E., 85
Smith, Miss Gertrude, xiv,
Smith and Grant, 38, 85, 86, 117
Smith, Hartley T., 109
Smith, J. W. W., 86
Smith and Kitts, 86
Smith, Nicholas, 87
Smith, Richard Ewing, ix, 24, 43, 51, 64, 70, 79, 85, 86, 87, 96, 101, 117
Smith, Sophie, 86
Smith, Steel, 87
Smith, Thomas, 87
Smith, W. C., 87
Smith, William, 87
Smith, William C., 87
Snyder, Catherine, 89
Snyder, Charlie, 89
Snyder, George, Sr., 7, 68, 76, 87, 88, 89, 118
Snyder, George Reynolds, 89
Snyder, George W., Jr., 87, 88, 89
Snyder, James C., 88, 89
Snyder, J. C. and G. W., 89
Snyder, Robert J., 89
Somer, Mrs., 33
Sowhey, Jacob, 20
Spear, Isaack, 62
Spears, Mr. Abram, 60
Spears, Mrs. Abram, 60
Spears, David H., 89
Speed Memorial Museum, J. B., 64
Speigelhalder, Ferdinand, 90, 118
Speigelhalder, John F., 90
Speigelhalder and Sons, 90
Speigelhalder and Werne, 90, 97
Spurgin, David M., 44, 49, 91

Stamps, Thomas, 88
Staples, Charles R., XX, 13, 42, 46
Starling, Miss Nannie K., xiv,
Steele, Adam, 91
Steele and Carr, 92
Steele, Miss Elizabeth, xiv, 41
Steele, John, 91
Steele, Joseph, 91
Steele, Martha, 91
Steele, Richard, 91
Steele, Robert, 75, 91
Steele, Robert M., 91
Steele, Rev. William, 91, 92
Steele, William, Jr., 92
Stephens, Joseph Lawrence, 72, 92, 94
Stewart, George W., vii, 93, 94, 106, 118
Stewart, William, 95
Stone, William R., 95
Stoy, David C., 95
"Sublimity," 38
Sutherland, Polly (Steele), 91
Sylmaris Collection, The, 14

Talbot, W. H., 109
Talbott, Aria, 41
Talbott, Aria Kennedy, 41
Talbott, Mrs. Rebecca J., xiv, 44
Talbott, W. H., and Company, 109
Taylor, Fayette, 55
Taylor, Martha J., 40
Taylor, Zachary, 55
Thirty-Second Kentucky Cavalry, C.S.A., 68
Thomas, Aria (Hinamon), 41
Thompson, Joseph S., 95
Thompson, Captain W. B., 59
Timberlake, Henry, 7
Timberlake, Mary, 7
Tobia, M. I., 94
Tod, L. L., 27, 50
Todd, Robert S., 15
Todd, William, 95, 96
Tomes, Francis, and Sons, 51
Tonkrey, Silas, 96
Townsend, William H., vii, xiv, 15
Transylvania College, xiii, 37
Trimble, Hon. Robert, 72

University of Kentucky Library, xiii,
Urban, Father, 19, 20, 36

Van Hoy, Shelby, 109
Van Hoy, Shelby S., Jr., 109
Van Hoy, Mrs. Shelby S., Jr., xiv, 109
Vaughn, Henry H., 99
Veeter, Anthony, 96
Verhoeff, Miss Mary, xiii, 74
Vest, John J., 68
Virney, ———, 96

Wait, Edgar S., 86, 96
Wakefield, Sarah Snyder (Mrs. John), xiv, 88, 89
Ward, Martha Jane, 60

Index

Warren, John, 6
Warriner, S. W., 2, 96
Washington, General George, 8
Weaks, Miss Mabel, xiv, 14, 105
Werne, Joseph, Jr., 54, 97
Werne, Joseph, Sr., 28, 54, 90, 97, 118
West, Edward, Jr., ix, x, 78, 97, 98, 99
West, Edward, Sr., 97
West, Elizabeth, 99
West, Elizabeth Mills, 97
West, Lewis, 99
West, Luther G., 85
West, Sarrah, 97, 99
West, William Edward, 97
Whitaker, Aquilla, 13
Whitaker, Elizabeth, 13
White, Peter, 100
White, Peter, Sr., 100
Whitley, Mrs. Wade Hampton, xiv, 1, 41, 54, 64, 75, 88, 89, 107
Wilkinson, General James, 37
Wilkinson, Samuel, 16
Williams, Susanna, 76
Williamson, John W., 80, 96
Willis, George L., Sr., 13

Wilson, Abner, 59
Wilson, Mr. and Mrs. Frank B., xiv,
Wilson, J., 100
Wilson, James, 100
Winchester, Daniel F., 23, 34, 36, 100
Wirt, John, 100
Wisdom, Mr., 41
Wolfe, George, 40
Wood, B. W., 48
Woodruff, Ezra, 78, 100
Woodruff, L. and E., 100
Woolley, John, 99
Woolridge, John W., 101
Wright, John F., 86, 101
Wright, Miss Sallie, 63
Wright, Dr. and Mrs. Walter, xiv,

Yale University School of Fine Arts, 64
Yeiser, Frederick, 101
Yeiser, F., and Company, 101
Yeiser, Philip, 101
Young, Thomas, 102
Young, Judge Thomas P., 30

Zumar, George A., 11, 102

www.ingramcontent.com/pod-product-compliance
Lightning Source LLC
Chambersburg PA
CBHW050323120526
44592CB00014B/2021